NOTES ON THE WOUNDED
FROM
THE MUTINY IN INDIA:
WITH
A DESCRIPTION OF THE PREPARATIONS
OF
GUNSHOT INJURIES
CONTAINED
IN THE MUSEUM AT FORT PITT.

BY
GEORGE WILLIAMSON, M. D.

GYAN

Published by

GYAN

Gyan Publishing House
5, Ansari Road
Daryaganj, New Delhi-110002
Phone: 011-47034999, 9811692060
E-mail: books@gyanbooks.com

Distribution Network
gyanbooks.com
India, USA, Canada, UK, Australia, France

ISBN: 978-81-212-7989-5 (PB)
First Published, 1859

2nd Impression 2023

Printed at: Gyan Press, Delhi.

NOTES ON THE WOUNDED FROM THE MUTINY IN INDIA
Author: GEORGE WILLIAMSON

NOTES ON THE WOUNDED FROM THE MUTINY IN INDIA

NOTES ON THE WOUNDED

FROM

THE MUTINY IN INDIA:

WITH

A DESCRIPTION OF THE PREPARATIONS

OF

GUNSHOT INJURIES

CONTAINED

IN THE MUSEUM AT FORT PITT.

BY

GEORGE WILLIAMSON, M. D.,

STAFF SURGEON.

LONDON:

JOHN CHURCHILL, NEW BURLINGTON-STREET.

1859.

PREFACE.

All Soldiers of Cavalry and Infantry of the Line, invalided on account of wounds, pass through the Invalid Depôt at Chatham.

It is there, then, that probably the best opportunity is to be found for ascertaining the results of different wars, in the several classes and species of wounds, and in the proportion which those classes and species bear to each other, and to the total by all wounds. The collection and record of such results seem to me to be always very desirable; and I have availed myself of the opportunity alluded to as regards the wounded by the mutiny in India. The following pages contain the result of my labours. I feel that they might have been made more valuable and interesting had similar accurate records existed of the invalids wounded by former wars, with which I could have compared data, and so have drawn more comprehensive information, statistical and surgical. I am in hopes, however, that some points worthy of notice have been elicited; and, for example, I may refer to the large number of cases of gunshot compound fracture of the femur, where the patients have recovered with good, useful limbs, as compared with the number of thigh-stump cases, and the total by all wounds.

This very satisfactory feature in the classified return of invalided wounded by the mutiny, appears to me perhaps not uncommon for Indian wars, but certainly very much so for European wars, as far as records enable me to make the comparison. This difference in favour of results by Indian wars I believe to be mainly due to the facilities afforded by the dooley for the successful treatment of this severest of all forms of compound fracture. 11 cases recovered, with good, useful limbs, out of the total wounded landed from India—viz., 743, or 1·49 per cent. This is a large proportion compared with the result of the Crimean war, viz., 8 out of 2296, or 0·34 per cent.

Medical officers who have served in India are, I believe, unanimous in opinion, that there is no means of transit for sick and wounded equal to the dooley; and should this be admitted by the public and the Government, there seems no reason why our Indian subjects should not furnish us with a supply of doolies and bearers in all our wars out of India. That such a means of transport would be expensive, must be admitted; but probably not so very much more expensive than the means usually supplied. The difference would not, I believe, be grudged by the public, who would find their satisfaction in the more favourable results amongst the severer classes of cases of invalided wounded arriving at the Depôt.

Advantage has been taken of the valuable preparations on this subject contained in the Museum of the Army Medical Department, to illustrate these notes. The specimens have been carefully described, and the history of the cases detailed as fully as possible, and several lithographic drawings have also been inserted. This, it is hoped, may be of some use, as informing the profession of what preparations of gunshot and other injuries received in action the Museum at Fort Pitt contains.

NOTES ON GUNSHOT INJURIES,

&c. &c.

THE wounded of the Cavalry and Infantry of the Line, consequent on the Mutiny in India, who have hitherto arrived in England, having been specially placed under my charge for observation, record, and report, as well as treatment when that was further necessary; and the arrangement of the specimens of gunshot and other injuries incidental to active military life, to be found in the Museum (at Fort Pitt), having at the same time occupied my attention; I am induced to believe, that from these two sources of information opportunities have occurred to me, of which the results may be useful to military medical officers, and not without interest to the profession generally. In the task of classification of those wounds and injuries received in action, I have to acknowledge, with thanks, the assistance of the principal medical officer at Fort Pitt, Inspector-General Taylor, C. B., whose classification[a], proposed during the Crimean War, has been adopted.

The following return, based on that classification, will be found to present a very concise summary of the nature of all the cases of gunshot and other injuries received in the actions occasioned by the Mutiny in India, and will serve at the same time as an index to the method I propose to pursue in submitting the remarks I have to make on the several varieties of gunshot wounds.

[a] A Classification of Wounds and Injuries received in action, proposed for use in Military Hospitals, by J. R. Taylor, C. B., Deputy Inspector-General, Camp before Sebastopol, June 25, 1856.

The men, on arrival from the long sea voyage from India, had recovered their general health, and the greater number of them had their wounds healed.

The tabular form, completed and closed up to the 31st of March, 1859, shows that the total number wounded which had arrived up to this date was 603; of these, 193 have been sent to duty; 67 to modified duty[a]; 263 invalided; 7 died; and 73 remain undisposed of.

Of the fatal cases since landing in England, 1 was a case of gunshot wound of the head,—cause of death, chronic hepatitis and ascites; 2 were cases of perforating gunshot wound of the lung,—1 of which died of gangrene of the opposite lung, and 1 of phthisis; 1 case of partial fracture of the humerus,—cause of death, pyemia; 1 case of compound comminuted fracture of the femur, ball lodged between the ends of the united fracture,—cause of death, chronic dysentery; 1 case of amputation of the arm,—death from gangrene of the stump; 1 case of amputation at the middle of the thigh,—cause of death, necrosis and exhaustion. Besides these, 1 case (an artilleryman) died at Gravesend, from gunshot fracture of the tibia, followed by sloughing, but not included in the return.

DESCRIPTIVE NUMERICAL RETURN *of Wounds and Injuries received in Action during the Mutiny in India, and the Sufferers from which were landed in England, at Fort Pitt, up to the 31st March,* 1859.

Classification and Specification of Wounds and Injuries.	Landed at Gravesend.	Discharged to Duty.	Discharged to Modified Duty.	Invalided.	Died.	Remaining undisposed.
1. Gunshot Wounds of the Head:—						
1. Contusions and simple flesh-wounds of the scalp, ...	2	2				
2. With contusion or fracture of the cranium, without depression, ...	5	3	. .	2		
3 Ditto, with depression, or displacement of both tables, ...	8	2	1	3	1	1
Total, . . .	15	7	1	5	1	1

[a] An order, dated 20th August, 1858, was received from the Assistant Adjutant-General, stating that men who had been wounded, and so far disabled as to be unfit for the active duties of a soldier, might still be very efficient as orderlies, messengers, clerks, &c., and were to be retained in the service for that purpose.

Classification and Specification of Wounds and Injuries.	Landed at Gravesend.	Discharged to Duty.	Discharged to Modified Duty.	Invalided.	Died.	Remaining undisposed.
2. Gunshot Wounds of the Face:—						
1. Simple flesh contusions and wounds, .	1	. .	. .	1		
2. Penetrating, perforating, or lacerating the bony structures, without lesion of important organs, ...	3	3				
3. Ditto, with lesion of the eye, ...	12	3	. .	7	. .	2
4. Ditto, with fracture of the lower jaw,	6	2	1	3		
Total, . . .	22	8	1	11	. .	2
3. Gunshot Wounds of the Neck:—						
1. Simple flesh contusions and wounds, .	7	6	. .	. .	. .	1
4. Gunshot Wounds of the Chest:—						
1. Simple flesh contusions and wounds, .	5	5				
2. With injury of bony or cartilaginous parietes, without lesion of contents, .	3	2	. .	1		
3. With lesion of contents by contusion, or with non-penetrating wound, . . .	2	2				
5. Perforating contents, ...	9	5	1	1	2	
Total, . . .	19	14	1	2	2	
5. Gunshot Wounds of the Abdomen:—						
1. Simple flesh contusions and wounds, .	4	4				
2. Contusion, or non-penetrating wound, with lesion of stomach, ...	2	2				
3. Penetrating or perforating, with lesion of intestine, ...	2	1	. .	. .	. .	1
Total, . . .	8	7	. .	. .	. .	1
6. Gunshot Wounds of Back and Spine:—						
1. Simple flesh contusions and wounds, .	3	2	. .	. .	. .	1
2. With fracture of vertebræ, without lesion of spinal cord, ...	6	2	. .	2	. .	2
Total, . . .	9	4	. .	2	. .	3
7. Gunshot Contusions and Wounds of the Perineum and Genital and Urinary Organs, not being at the same time Wounds of the Peritoneum, ...	3	2	. .	. .	. .	1
8. Gunshot Wounds of the Upper Extremities:—						
1. Simple flesh contusions and wounds, slight, ...	39	30	6	6	. .	5
" " severe,	8					
2. With contusion and partial fracture of long bones, including fracture of the clavicle and scapula, ...	30	13	4	5	1	7
3. Simple fracture of long bones by contusion from round shot, ...	2	. .	. .	2		
Forward,	79	43	10	13	1	12

Classification and Specification of Wounds and Injuries.	Landed at Gravesend.	Discharged to Duty.	Discharged to Modified Duty.	Invalided.	Died.	Remaining undisposed.
Brought forward,	79	43	10	13	1	12
8. Gunshot Wounds of the Upper Extremities:—						
4. With compound fracture of humerus, .	17	. .	3	13	. .	1
,, ,, radius, ...	18	1	2	14	. .	1
,, ,, ulna, ...	7	2	1	3	. .	1
,, ,, ulna and radius,	3	1	. .	2		
5. Penetrating, perforating, or lacerating the several structures of the carpus and metacarpus, ...	26	5	7	13	. .	1
6. Dividing or lacerating the structures of the fingers and thumbs, ...	9	4	. .	2	. .	3
Total, . . .	159	56	23	60	1	19
9. Gunshot Wounds of the Lower Extremities:—						
1. Simple flesh contusions and wounds, slight, ...	87	63	6	13	. .	18
,, ,, severe,	13					
2. With contusion and partial fracture of long bones, or of the bones of the pelvis in their relation to the lower extremities, ...	28	8	4	10	. .	6
4. With compound fracture of femur, . .	8	. .	2	5	1	
,, ,, tibia only, . .	6	. .	1	5		.
,, ,, fibula only, . .	4	3	. .	1		
,, ,, tibia and fibula,	2	. .	. .	2		
5. Penetrating, perforating, or lacerating the several structures of the tarsus and metatarsus, ...	13	4	2	5	. .	2
6. Dividing or lacerating the structure of the toes, ...	1	. .	1			
Total, . . .	162	78	16	41	1	26
10. Gunshot Wounds with direct penetration or perforation of the larger Joints, with Fracture of Bone, ...	8	. .	. .	5	. .	3
,, ,, without Fracture,	1	. .	. .	1		
Total, . . .	9	. .	. .	6	. .	3
11. Gunshot Wounds with direct Injury of large Nerves, not being at the same time Cases of Compound Fracture, ...	6	. .	. .	3	. .	3
12. Sword and Lance Wounds, ...	12	5	1	6		
13. Bayonet Wounds, ...	2	1	. .	. .	. .	1
14. Miscellaneous Wounds and Injuries received in Action, ...	9	2	1	3	. .	3
Total Wounds and Injuries received in Action,	442	190	44	139	5	64

Return *of Capital Operations.*

Description of Operation.	Landed at Gravesend.	Discharged to Duty.	Discharged to Modified Duty.	Invalided.	Died.	Remaining undisposed.
Amputations.						
Upper extremities.						
Shoulder-joint,	6	. .	. .	6		
Arm,	46	. .	3	40	1	2
Forearm,	19	. .	1	17	. .	1
Thumbs,	12	1	5	5	. .	1
Fingers,	41	1	12	26	. .	2
Lower Extremities.						
Thigh, at upper third,	1	. .	. .	1		
,, middle third,	10	. .	. .	8	1	1
Leg,	18	. .	. .	17	. .	1
Ankle-joint,	1	. .	. .	1		
Medio-tarsus,	2	. .	. .	2		
Toes,	2	1	. .	. .	. .	1
Total,	158	3	21	123	2	9
Excisions.						
Upper Extremities.						
Shoulder-joint,	1	. .	1			
Elbow-joint.	2	. .	2			
Total,	3	. .	3			
Ligature of Arteries, included under other Heads.						
Brachial,	1					
Radial,	1					
Post Tibial,	1					
Total,	3					
Total Amputations and Excisions,	161	3	23	124	2	9
Total Wounds and Injuries received in Action,	442	190	44	139	5	64
Total Wounded landed at Gravesend,	603	193	67	263	7	73

This is probably nearly the total number that will arrive from the Mutiny in India; only a very few more can now be expected.

Class I.—Gunshot Wounds of the Head.

Division 1.—*Contusions and simple Flesh Wounds of the Scalp.*

2 were admitted, and were sent to duty.

DIVISION 2.— *With Contusion or Fracture of the Cranium, without Depression.*

5 were admitted, of whom 3 were sent to duty, and 2 invalided for other diseases. In all of them, small portions of the external tables of the skull came away, necrosed. The scalp was not adherent to the bone in any of them.

The brain and meninges appear readily to support loss of bone by caries and necrosis, and to accommodate themselves to a denudation of osseous covering, which takes place gradually; whilst forcible removal by gunshot injury and operation is more generally resented.

The following cases are good examples of this tolerance of loss of bone caused by necrosis.

No. 2895. Three portions of necrosed parietal bone; the sequestra embrace the entire thickness of the bone. The number of square inches of bone removed is about 5½ inches; they were taken from the superior and posterior angles of both parietal bones. See Plate I., fig. 1.

From Thomas Walker, 95th Regiment. This is an example of extensive contusion from gunshot wound of the vertex, followed by necrosis, and ultimate recovery, without the use of the trephine at any stage during the treatment.

The following preparation from Private G. Bookland, 23rd Regiment, is a case of contusion from a portion of shell without any external wound. Eight months after the injury he was insensible for twenty-one days, but gradually recovered consciousness. The trephine was, however, ultimately applied over the vertex, and the outer table, with portions of the internal table, were removed, and a large quantity of matter was evacuated. The patient recovered.

No. 2896. A large sequestrum, about six inches in diameter, composed almost entirely of the external table of both parietal bones. There are only two small portions, which include both tables. There is an opening in the bone made by the trephine for the evacuation of matter.

No. 3626. Necrosed portions of the bones of the cranium, about two inches in length, and one and a half in breath, consisting of the whole thickness of the skull; the lambdoidal suture runs through its centre. The piece is composed of part of the occipital and part of the parietal bones. There are also two smaller portions: one of them is of the whole thickness, and the other of the outer table only. From M'Gifford; an Indian case, page 11.

No. 2910. This cranium shows large irregular depressions and various degrees of deficiency of its parietes, in some places comprehending both tables, and in others the external only, and chiefly affecting the left side. The exposed surface of the inner table is quite smooth and compact, as well as the margins of the depressions.

This was the effect of various exfoliations succeeding to a sabre wound of the left parietal bone. The patient was an African negro, a maniac, with occasional violent paroxysms. Disease of four years' duration.

I may also mention the following case, although it was not the result of gunshot wound[a]:—

No. 3176. A cast in wax exhibiting a greater extent of disease affecting the bones of the cranium than perhaps any other case on record, without in any way producing injury to the general health or cerebral functions. The greater portion of the vault of the skull has been removed, and there does not appear to have been the least reproduction of new bone; still, the brain in this case, when last examined by me, was, to a great extent, protected by the effusion of fibrinous matter and consolidation of parts, so as at some places to prevent the pulsation of the brain from being felt,—as has been more fully insisted upon under Division 3.

The disease, necrosis and caries, commenced in T. Blackman, a sailor, in 1845, the result of a fall on board ship. He is now, 1859, in robust health, suffering but little inconvenience from the extent of disease. He is at present an orderly in the Melville Hospital, Chatham[b].

Fracture of the inner or vitreous table of the skull, without fracture or depression of the outer, is of very rare occurrence; still, such an accident may take place, as the following case shows[c]:—

This case proved fatal from compression of the cerebral substance. The question arises,—would this compression have been relieved by the operation of trephining. I believe not, and for the following reasons: first, that the compressing medium was not a fluid which might have escaped through an aperture in the cranium, but coagulated blood; and, secondly, to have operated, and punctured the dura mater when this membrane was in a state of inflammation, would have greatly

[a] This case has been described by Dr. Drummond, D. I. G.

[b] Every case here recorded is the result of a gunshot wound, except when stated to the contrary. The descriptions of the preparations are in general alone given, with a short notice of the result of the case: reference can be made, when required, for further details to the Museum Catalogue.

[c] See the remarks on this subject in Mr. Guthrie's Commentaries, paragraph 262, Lecture xviii.; and Hennen's Military Surgery, p. 326, last edition, 1829.

increased the chances of a fatal issue. The case is interesting, as showing an injury of the internal table of the skull, unconnected with any lesion of the external, and produced by a ball whose conical shape and sharp apex would have led one to expect quite the opposite injury, viz., fracture of the external table and uninjured internal.

May we not also suspect that other cases of this description of fracture have occurred, and have not been observed on post-mortem examination, as took place in this instance, the fissure not being remarked until the calvarium was macerated.

No. 2893.—Calvarium showing a distinct fissure, limited to the internal table, running parallel to the course which the ball had taken, with commencing necrosis. Death in thirteen days after the receipt of the wound.—*Donor, Mr. Cowan, Assistant Surgeon, 55th Regiment.* This specimen was taken from Private James Burke, 55th Regiment, aged 19, who walked home from the trenches, and was admitted into hospital Aug. 24, 1855. He said that when at the rear a musket-ball, which he found afterwards, struck him on the head. On examination a distinct linear slit, about three inches long, and running parallel with the axis of the brain, was observed situated over the upper surface of the right parietal bone. On introducing the finger, the bone was found quite bare, but no fracture or depression could be discovered.

There were no general symptoms of any serious injury of the head. The head was ordered to be shaved, and cold water dressing applied.

August 29th. Had been progressing favourably until this evening, when the whole scalp was observed to be swollen, but not at all reddened. The œdema was greatest on the right side of the head and face. The edges of the wound looked unhealthy and green, and there was a peculiar smell from the wound; he complained of a want of power in his left arm; the muscles of the face were slightly twisted towards the right side; he could move his legs freely; a crucial incision was made through the wound, the flaps retracted, and the bone carefully examined.

No injury of its intimate structure could be detected, but a distinct black line marked the course of the ball; the pulse was small and weak; numerous free incisions were made here and there over the swollen scalp; from these wounds a great deal of serum escaped.

August 30th. Symptoms of hemiplegia were more distinct; œdema of the scalp quite gone; wound looks more healthy; the bone appeared dead.

September 5th. Had one slight convulsion this morning; respiration decidedly more hurried; in consultation no operation was deemed advisable; had been put under the influence of mercurials.

September 6th. Was much weaker; respiration decidedly more hurried; has had another convulsion; died comatose in the evening.

Post-mortem Examination, eight hours after death.—Calvarium firmly adherent beneath the seat of this injury. On removing it, a false membrane was observed on the dura mater, corresponding exactly to the parietal protuberance, and measuring about two inches in diameter; vessels of dura mater and pia mater congested; underneath the dura mater, at the spot to which the false membrane was adherent, was a large clot of coagulated blood, of the size of a walnut, distinctly circumscribed, and extending in depth to the roof of the lateral ventricle of the same hemisphere. Portions of this clot were degenerated into a reddish grumous matter, possessing no consistence. The cerebral substance around was softened; the other hemisphere of brain was quite healthy; no effusion in either of the ventricles; the internal aspect of the calvarium *seemed at first quite sound*, but after the bone was macerated, a distinct fissure, limited to the internal table, running parallel to the course of the ball, and about half an inch in length, was perceived; the other organs of the body were healthy.

Division 3.—*With Contusion or Fracture of the Cranium, with Depression or Displacement of both Tables.*

Eight cases of this description of fracture arrived from India, and are good examples of fracture of the cranium, and displacement of both tables, with exposure and probable injury to the dura mater. In all of them there was a depressed and generally an adherent cicatrix, which plainly showed that there had been extensive injury and loss of bone, but in none of the cases, on their examination at Fort Pitt, about twelve months after the receipt of the wound, could the pulsation of the brain be felt, the parts having had time to contract and become consolidated by the effusion of a strong fibrous substance.

The size and extent of the depression in the bone, or certain sensorial symptoms remaining, were sufficient evidence that the contents of the cranium had been exposed. It is well known that the bones of the cranium have very little power of repairing injuries inflicted in their continuity by throwing out new osseous matter, but it does not appear to have been noticed or insisted on, that nature seems to make up for this, by the gradual contraction and filling up of the loss of substance by the deposition of fibrous matter and the gradual contraction and consolidation of the injured parts, so as to effectually close in and protect the brain. This process is well exemplified in some of the cases of gunshot wounds that have arrived from India.

Besides these cases, Dr. Smith, Assistant Surgeon, 9th Lancers, who served with the army at the siege of Delhi, informed me that Captain R. of the Carbineers, and Captain E. of the 60th Rifles, both now in England, are instances of the reparative process just mentioned.

The dura mater was more or less exposed, and the pulsation of the brain visible in both these officers, but in neither, for some months past, has the pulsation been observable, on account of the effusion of fibrous matter and gradual contraction and consolidation of the perforated parts.

In several instances perfectly loose and displaced pieces of bone appear to have been removed, but in none of the cases is there any evidence or even suspicion of trephining having been performed.

After removing any loose or detached portions of bone, the expectant prophylactic treatment seems to be the one usually followed in the present day, and considered to be the most successful.

Nos. 2884, 2885, 2886, 2894, are good examples of this kind of fracture, showing the appearance of parts some considerable time after the receipt of the wound, as also those cases from India of recovery from this injury without the use of the trephine.

With regard to the mode of dressing in gunshot wounds of the head, a piece of fine wet linen is first applied, which adheres to the wound, and should not be frequently removed. Over this, Stromeyer recommends that a net, made for the purpose, should be placed, so as to retain the dressing, and the cold applications are to be made through the net. Patients labouring under wounds of the head are frequently so restless that the wet lint is quickly tossed off, so that the suggestion of Stromeyer appears to be worthy of being generally adopted.

93rd Regt.—Private Jas. Campbell, aged 19.—Wounded at Lucknow, 16th November, 1857, by a musket-ball, which struck him in the centre of the forehead close to the root of the hair, and caused a compound comminuted fracture of the frontal bone; several pieces of bone have come away.

July 10, 1858. The wound is now healed; there is a depression at the seat of injury, about the size of a cherry, where all the tables of the skull appear to be removed, although the pulsation of the brain cannot be felt, and he complains of severe pain in the head. The man states that the ball is still in the head, and that the medical officers in India inserted the probe for several inches along the inner surface of the bone, and found the ball, but could not extract it.

Invalided, 9th August, 1858.

64th Regiment.—Private Matthew M'Glasher, aged 39, twenty-two years' service.

Wounded on the 12th of August, 1857, by a portion of shell at the storming of Bassack Gungee in Oude; it struck him on the upper part of the left side of the forehead, at the upper and outer angle of the frontal bone, a portion of which was taken away two days after the wound.

June 11, 1858. There are now two long cicatrices leading down to a deep depression capable of holding a marble, resulting from the loss of apparently all the tables of the skull, although the pulsation of the brain cannot be felt. He is in good health, and free from headach, except when he exposes himself to the sun, or stoops, &c.

September 3, 1858. Was sent to modified duty.

3rd Battn. R. B.—Private Charles Brown. Wounded at Cawnpore, December 6, 1857, by a musket-ball between the eyes into the frontal sinus; it was extracted forty-eight hours after. Several pieces of bone have come away.

July 12th. The wound is now nearly closed, there being only a small aperture capable of admitting a probe in the centre of a small depression; bare bone cannot be felt, and there is almost no discharge from it, and he is free from headach.

September 11, 1858. Duty.

37th Regt.—Private John M'Gifford.—Wounded 30th July, 1857, by a musket-ball in the head; the ball passed across the upper part of the occiput, severely injuring the bone, which was left quite bare; one large piece of necrosed bone, the whole thickness, came away about three months after. Preparation No. 3626, page 6.

July 16, 1858. Wound healed; there is now a deep depression, about three inches in length, across the upper part of the occipital bone; also a deep groove leading down from the centre of the first depression in the form of the letter T; always complains of pains in the head and giddiness.

July 17, 1858. Invalided.

34th Regt.—Private Thomas Long. Wounded at Cawnpore, November 26, 1857, on the left temple, by a piece of shell, which lacerated the scalp and fractured the outer table of the parietal bone; necrosis ensued, and two small pieces of bone have come away.

July 14, 1858. Wound healed; there is a deep depression, about three inches in length, capable of holding a finger, from loss of the outer table and probable depression of the inner; complains of headach.

August 6, 1858. Invalided.

53rd Regt.—Private John O'Donnell. Wounded at Cawnpore, December 6, 1857, by a musket-ball, which struck him on the head a little to the left of the sagittal suture on the upper and back part of the left parietal bone, close to that suture; ball extracted immediately after; exfoliation of bone took place.

July 13, 1858. Wound healed; there is now a deep depression capable of holding a cherry; the whole thickness of the skull seems to have come away, still the pulsation of the brain cannot be felt; complains of pain in the head; remains undisposed of.

78th Regt.—Private John Halliday received a gunshot wound in the head whilst on service in Oude, in July, 1857. The slugs, or pieces of telegraph wire, with which the wound was inflicted, struck the left parietal bone near the temporal ridge, carrying away a large portion of the scalp and bone; other pieces of bone have been extracted since the receipt of the wound, leaving a large irregular opening about two inches in diameter, through which the brain may be seen pulsating; mental faculties clear; has shown no symptoms of cerebral excitement; the immediate cause of death was chronic hepatitis and ascites.

Died May 29, 1858, at Gravesend.

Post Mortem.—General appearance of Body.—Abdomen and scrotum distended with fluid; both legs and feet very œdematous; a large cicatrix on the left side of the head, about three inches above and behind the ear. *Head.*—On removing the scalp over the wounded part, a small quantity of bloody pus oozed from around a small portion of necrosed bone near the temporal suture, and an opening in the skull was exposed, about the size of a shilling, having a fibrous covering, which alone separated the brain from a thin cicatrix of scalp. The edges of the opening were cartilaginous, and the bone around was rough and irregular; a considerable portion of the adjoining outer table of the skull was apparently carried away at the time he was wounded.

The following specimen shows the result of a severe contusion and fracture from a round shot, with slight depression

Pl. I.

Fig. 1.

2895

Fig. 2.

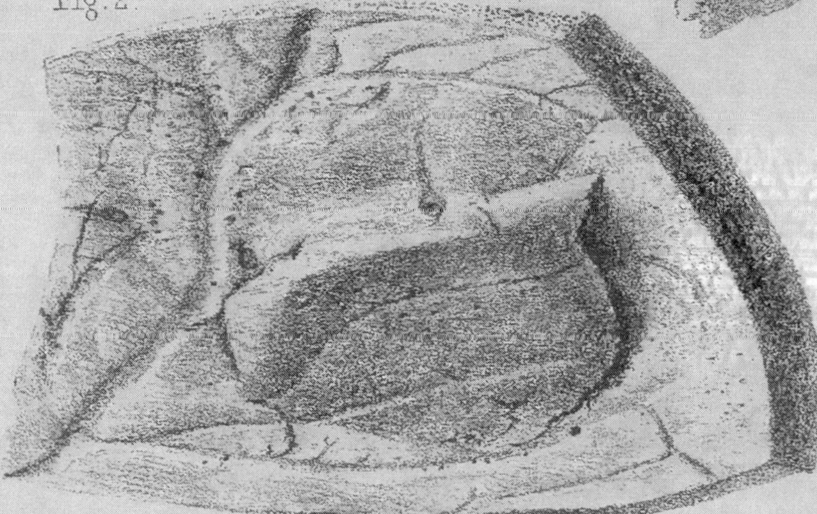

2885

Fig. 3.

2905

Fig. 4.

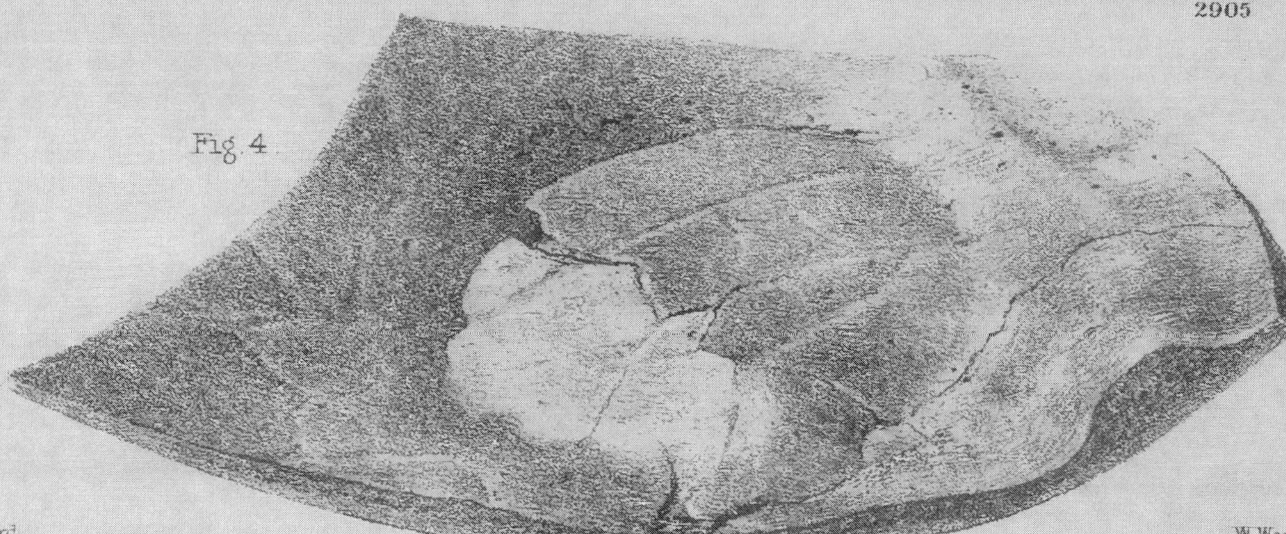

2894

G H Ford. W West imp.

of the internal table, five and a half years after the injury, with actual bony union of displaced fragments, and a depression of the contents of the cranium.

No. 2884. Portion of the left parietal bone, showing the result of a gun-shot fracture. A portion of bone exfoliated, and there is now a depression in the external table, and corresponding to this there is a depressed fragment of the internal table, with smooth edges, which is reunited by new bony matter to the old bone. This specimen was taken from Private William Freeman, 80th Regiment, aged 35, who received a severe contusion of the head by a gunshot, at Ferozeshah, December 22, 1845. When first under notice, there was no disturbance of the sensorial functions, and no breach of the scalp, but great tumefaction of the parts from ecchymosis; suppuration and exfoliation followed. The patient recovered perfectly, and neither then nor afterwards did he appear to have suffered cerebral symptoms in consequence of the wound. Died June 16, 1851, of dysentery.

On post-mortem examination, there was a slight depression in the cerebral substance and membranes of the brain, opposite to the fracture, which had a darker and more vascular appearance than elsewhere, but there was no thickening or trace of lymph.—*Donor, J. R. Taylor, Surgeon, 80th Regt.*

No. 2885.—From Private D. Mullens, 36th Regiment. Shows a depressed fracture of right parietal bone; it projects to a considerable extent internally, and new bone is thrown out around it. The margins of the fracture are smooth and rounded off, and reunited to the old bone.—*Donor, Dr. Russell, Surgeon, 36th Regt.* This is a good example of a considerable depressed fracture, without a single bad symptom, and complete recovery taking place in the short space of a fortnight, without the use of the trephine. See Plate I., Fig. 2.

No. 2886 —Skull-cap, exhibiting an old reunited fracture of the frontal bone. The inner table is considerably depressed, without corresponding depression of the outer. From a soldier who was wounded in the head in Spain, several years before his death.

This specimen shows well how much the inner table is broken and depressed, compared to the outer, and the appearance after many years.

The following is one of those obscure cases of injury of the head where, immediately after the receipt of the injury, there is no relation between the symptoms developed and the actual extent of the lesion. There must have been a large extravasation of blood in the left hemisphere, immediately on the receipt of the wound; and yet the patient was able to walk home, a distance of two miles, and not the slightest symptom of paralysis was discoverable.

No. 2888.—Calvarium showing fracture of the left parietal bone, caused by a shell. The depressed portions of bone were removed, and the dura mater punctured to allow purulent matter to escape. —*Donor, Mr. Cowan, Assistant Surgeon, 55th Regiment.* This specimen was taken from Private D. O'Leary, 55th Regiment, who was wounded by a portion of shell at the assault on the Redan, September 8, 1855. From the fact of there not being the slightest general symptoms of compression, cold dressing was applied, and the case minutely watched.

September 11th. Complained of headach and sickness at the stomach. A crucial incision was at once made through the wound; the portion of bone depressed was found to include both tables; that of the external was fractured, while that of the internal was merely depressed. The opening left was about the size of a shilling; the dura mater at once protruded through the aperture, and was punctured, when a reddish, semi-purulent matter escaped. The patient after the operation stated that he felt no pain, and fell into a deep sleep.

14th. Had a convulsive fit, and an excessive action of the muscles of the face and neck.

15th. Complete paralysis of right side; he was insensible; there was a true hernia cerebri.

16th. Died, comatose.

Calvarium firmly adherent; dura mater discoloured, and softened round the seat of injury; the whole of left hemisphere presented one mass of blood, and disorganized cerebral matter.

The next preparation, from Sergeant Shea, 49th Regiment, shows how a patient may recover so far from a depressed and comminuted fracture of the skull as to be able to go about and to all appearance to be in tolerably good health for fifty-four days after the accident, until suddenly seized with convulsions. It is questionable whether this man would have had a better chance had the trephine been applied, and the depressed bone raised, on the receipt of the injury. Subsequently, when the patient was in such good health, there was every prospect of his ultimate recovery, and a surgeon under these circumstances would have had considerable hesitation in recommending an operation, and most likely the patient could not have seen any necessity for having a hole made in his skull.

No. 2894.—Depressed fracture of the posterior part of the

right parietal bone. A sharp margin of the bone must have pressed to a great extent on the dura mater and brain. See Plate I., Fig. 4.

Out of 15 cases of this description of fracture that occurred in the Crimea, and are recorded in the Museum Catalogue, 4 were not operated on, and, of these, 3 died of abscess of the brain, and 1 recovered. Of 11 operated upon in consequence of symptoms of compression or inflammation, and to remove balls, 4 recovered, and 7 died. In the 15 cases, none of them had head symptoms for some days after being wounded, and none were operated upon before the fourth day, and 1 as late as the twenty-sixth day, and consequently after inflammatory symptoms had shown themselves.

The following are examples of some of the cases where the trephine or Hey's saw was employed.

No. 2900.—Shows the portion removed by the trephine from Private Leary, 18th Regiment.

In this case the fracture was on the right parietal bone, and paralysis of the left side of the face followed, the result of suppuration in the substance of the right hemisphere and membrane of the brain. Trephined four days after he was wounded, and died seven days after the operation.

The following specimen, from Private Conolly, 1st Battalion Rifles, shows a compound comminuted fracture of the frontal bone in the situation of the frontal sinuses. The internal table is considerably more splintered than the outer, and a portion of the bone appears to have been taken away by Hey's saw, to facilitate the removal of the loose pieces of bone.

No. 2892.—Calvarium, showing fracture and depression of the frontal bone, caused by a shell. The fracture is situated on the left side, immediately above the superciliary ridge. Three small pieces of bone were removed from the wound by operation.

No. 2901.—Portion of fractured bone removed by Hey's saw, from Private John Evans, Royal Artillery, who received three small lacerated wounds of the scalp by the blowing up of a magazine, and lay insensible for some time. The wounds healed, and he walked about, apparently well, until about a month after the receipt of the wound, when he became comatose, and on examining the head there appeared a small tumour which presented the characteristics of Potts' puffy tumour.

The symptoms of compression were relieved by operation, and ultimate recovery took place. This preparation and the two following, also No. 2900, were presented by Dr. Jephson, Surgeon, King's Dragoon Guards.

No. 2905.—Shows several large portions of bone removed by the trephine at two applications of the instrument, from Private D. M'Kenzie, 55th Regiment. See Plate I., Fig. 3.

In this case the symptoms of inflammation of the brain and its membranes set in, and he was trephined on the fourth day after being wounded. A large piece of bone turned edgewise, pressing down the dura mater nearly an inch, required a second application of the trephine; almost instant relief was obtained, and the patient ultimately recovered, and was discharged to duty six weeks after the receipt of the injury.

The following preparation, from Private C. Hancock, 21st Regiment, is an example of a depressed fracture from grape-shot. Inflammatory symptoms, with excruciating pain in the head, and double vision, came on. The trephine was applied on the fifth day after being wounded. Death took place on the sixteenth day.

2898.—Two very large portions of depressed fracture removed by the operation of trephining; thus illustrating the extensive injury inflicted by grape, and the comminuted fracture which is the result.

There are also other preparations in the Museum illustrating the removal or forcible elevation of depressed bone from Collins, Scribbins, Perry, and Perkins, whose cases are detailed in the second volume of the Medical and Surgical History of the British Army in the Crimea.

DIVISION 4.—*Penetrating and perforating the Cranium and its Contents.*

None were admitted under this head from India.

Unfortunately, men's heads are not what they used to be, or modern missiles are more deadly, for recent wars furnish not one exception to the fatal consequences of this species of wounds. Of 91 cases of penetrating and perforating gunshot wounds of the head, admitted into hospital in the Crimea between the 1st April, 1855, and the end of the war, all, without exception, proved fatal. The details of these cases, had they been given, would, however, have been instructive as showing that what are called symptoms of compression occur equally when a portion of cranium and brain is shot away, and the cerebral substance left without cover and support. Mr. Hennen notes the case of a soldier who had nearly half of the roof of the skull blown off by the bursting of a shell, and who had no untoward symptoms till the tenth day, when the brain got into a fungous state, and protruded to a great extent, and

(Mr. Hennen adds in italics) "*he died comatose, with all the symptoms of compression*"[a].

Leaden balls are generally flattened by striking against the bone; sometimes they are cut in two, one portion of which lodges, and the other flies off (2883) at various angles, according to the obliquity of the projectile force, &c., or it may remain under the scalp at the margin of the aperture, while the other portion enters the cranium (2891).

The following is a good example of a perforating gunshot wound of the skull, and shows extremely well the usual characters of the aperture at the entrance and exit of a musket-ball. The outer margin of the entrance of the ball is seen to be smooth, and its inner surface larger and more irregular, and (in this case only slightly) splintered; the internal table being generally splintered to a greater extent than the outer, which is thought to be owing to its being more brittle. The entrance and exit of the ball in this skull show that this appearance is rather produced by the injury proceeding from without inwards, and also from the force of the ball becoming less in passing through the outer table.

No. 2881.—Skull-cap, exhibiting two perforations made by a pistol-ball in the anterior and right side of the frontal bone, and in the posterior part of the left parietal bone. The ball entered in the former situation, and lodged in the latter. The first opening is round and smooth; the second is regular on the inner table, but the outer is torn up to an extent much larger than the ball, which is lodged in front of the splinters. From an officer who was killed in a duel.

The following specimen shows the result of a gunshot fracture, where the patient survived fifteen weeks after the injury. It is to be presumed that any loose splintered pieces of bone (if any existed) were removed by the surgeon, and in all probability other portions were driven into the brain along with the ball; still, the man lived for some time, and became convalescent, with the ball in the lateral ventricle. The internal surface of the bone shows marks of vascular action, with slight osseous deposit around the opening. Three large wormian bones are seen in the preparation, and the gunshot hole is through two of them.

No. 2882.—Portion of a cranium in which is a circular perforation made by a musket-ball at Waterloo. The external margin of the hole is sharp, but the internal is rounded off, and of somewhat larger diameter than the former. The ball lodged

[a] Hennen's Military Surgery, p. 353. Last Edition, 1829.

in the brain. The man, however, became convalescent, until he was attacked with apoplexy fifteen weeks after the wound, and died. The ball was found loose in the lateral ventricles, having shifted its original position.

The next preparation, from Private William Doyle, 19th Regiment, is very interesting, and shows:—1st. That a ball may be cut in two by striking the margin of the fractured bone, and in such a manner as to leave a smooth surface on the ball, as if it had been cut by a sharp instrument, and one portion of bullet to enter the cranium, causing fracture, depression, and splintering of the internal table. 2nd. That in all probability the depressed portion sprung up or was forced up by the motion and resistance caused by the brain. 3rd. That a bullet may enter the cranium without leaving an aperture in the skull, but merely a slight depression and fissure, and leaving no evidence of its having entered the skull during life, until found on post-mortem examination. 4th. That the internal table is more splintered than the external. 5th. That the trephine may be applied without the surgeon being able to take away splintered portions, or to find the ball; in this case, however, there was no evidence of a ball having penetrated. 6th. It also records a wound in the superior longitudinal sinus, with extravasation of blood on the brain. It also shows that the want of an apparently sufficient opening does not prove that the ball has not penetrated and lodged, as the elasticity of bone is such as to diminish the aperture to a considerable extent. The patient survived the wound five or six hours only.

No. 2883.—Lodgment of part of a rifle-ball in the brain, without the usual evidence of a hole in the cranium. Portion of cranium with a depressed fracture by musket-ball. Portion removed by trephine. Portion of rifle-ball found in cerebrum.—*Donor, T. Longmore, Surgeon, 19th Regiment.*

No. 2889.—Calvarium, showing the great extent of injury inflicted on the osseous substance by a conical musket-ball, which perforated the cranium. Not only are both openings joined by a well-defined fissure, but there are cracks radiating in all directions from both wounds.—*Donor, Mr. Cowan, Assistant Surgeon, 55th Regiment.*

This is from Private R. Davis, 55th Regiment. It is curious that portions of the bone large enough to allow of the easy introduction of the finger were removed, which had been driven before the ball and escaped with it through the aperture of exit; only a few loose spiculæ were found in the substance of the brain itself.

The ball in the case of Private Thomas Cain, Rifles, was split, and penetrated the dura mater and brain to the extent of an inch, and was extracted twenty-four days after the wound was received, and the depressed bone was elevated on the twenty-sixth day. There was an extensive abscess in the right lobe of the brain, and pus on the surface and in the ventricles, with fungus preventing the escape of the matter.

No. 2902.—Shows the portions of bone removed by the trephine, and also the musket-ball, split.

The following is a gunshot wound of the face and base of the skull; death ten days after the injury, from hemorrhage from the internal carotid, splinters of bone in the left hemisphere, and suppuration.

No. 2880.—Cranium, exhibiting the track of a musket-ball, from the lower and inner side of the right orbit to the carotid canal, in the petrous portion of the left temporal bone. The internal carotid artery was ruptured, and the ball lay near the opening; spiculæ of bone were entangled in the substance of the left hemisphere of the brain, and suppuration had commenced in this part.

No. 3197.—Cast of the head of a man who received a gunshot wound in the right anterior lobe of the brain when attempting suicide.

From Private Daniel Tonson, 24th Regiment. This is a good example of a gunshot wound penetrating the substance of the brain, with recovery without any operative measures.

SABRE OR BAYONET WOUNDS.

The cut by a sword or by any clean-cutting instrument occasionally produces a mere solution of continuity, and in some cases it causes a fracture or fissure, which extends further than the part actually cut by the sword.

No. 2909.—Calvarium of an officer of the 98th Regiment, who was killed at Peshawur. There is a large, deep cut through the upper part of the right parietal bone, extending into the left; the blow seems to have been from behind, and a second blow, or cut, seems to have taken away a portion of bone immediately below the other. Death 22 days after the injury.

Wounds of the *orbit* are always very dangerous on account of the close proximity of the brain, and are usually produced by any sharp-pointed weapon, such as a bayonet or sword, by a walking-cane or tobacco-pipe, penetrating the thin superior wall of the orbit, and entering the brain, causing inflammation and abscess. The orbital plate of the frontal bone and the ethmoid are very thin and fragile, and the anterior lobes of the brain can easily be reached either from the nostrils or orbits, and a wound in either of these situations may even take place without exciting the suspicion of the surgeon that any serious injury has been inflicted, until symptoms of inflammation of the brain set in, more especially as the wound externally may appear of a very trivial character, as occurred in the following case:—

No. 2794.—The bones of the face, and a portion of the cranium, with the broken extremity of a cane which had penetrated into the nostril at the left ala of the nose, and entered the inside of the skull immediately below the left optic nerve, carrying before it the left posterior clinoid process.—*Donor, Dr. Anderson, Surgeon, 12th Royal Lancers.*

Trumpeter E. Grainger, 12th Lancers; death two days after the accident[a].

CLASS II.—WOUNDS OF THE FACE.

DIVISION 1.—*Simple Flesh Contusions and Wounds*

Only one was admitted, and was invalided for diarrhœa.

DIVISION 2.—*Penetrating, perforating, or lacerating the Bony Structure, without lesion of important organs.*

Three cases were admitted from India, and were discharged to duty. One was a case of partial fracture of the lower jaw; two of the upper jaw, in one of which the ball made its exit through the palate into the mouth seven weeks after.

No. 2955. Cast of the breech and screw of a fowling-piece which lodged in the forehead and nasal cavities. From an officer, who lived seven years after the accident. The anterior portion of the right hemisphere of the brain rested on the flat part of the breech, and was separated only from it by a false membrane.

DIVISION 3.—*Penetrating, perforating, or lacerating the Bony Structure, with lesion of the Eye.*

12 were admitted from India with lesion of the eye, of which 3 were sent to duty and 7 invalided; 1 was a case of total loss of vision of both eyes; 8 had lost the right eye; and 3 the left; 7 were supplied with artificial eyes. The 3 sent to duty had lost the right eye, and had artificial eyes supplied to them. The injury to the eyes was caused by musket-ball

[a] For a full account of this case, with an illustration, see Dublin Quarterly Journal, vol. xi., p. 347.

in 8 instances, in 2 by a piece of shell, and in 2 by small shot. The musket-ball generally entered the temples, passed in a slanting direction, and made its exit through the eye.

The men supplied with artificial eyes were very much improved in appearance; and the different shades of colours of the iris and sclerotic were so well matched that it was almost impossible to tell the natural from the artificial one: so much was this the case, that the officers, on going down the ranks, were puzzled to know the one from the other; one man, in a drunken spree, had his eye broken to pieces, fortunately for him, without any injury from the broken portions of the artificial eye.

84th Regt.—Private Francis Lyons[a], wounded September 25, 1857, by a musket-ball, which entered the left temple in front of the ear, and passed out through the eye; two pieces of bone were taken away, two hours after, from the aperture of entrance of the ball.

January 11th. The sight of the eye is now entirely destroyed; the eyelid remains entire; there is a hollow in the left temple from the loss of bone and muscle; the wounds are healed; complains of pain in the head. Remains undisposed of.

93rd Regt.—Private Christopher Porter[a], wounded November 16, 1857, at Lucknow, by a small rifle-ball, which entered the left orbit at the side of the nose, and passed across the right orbit, and out about the centre of the right zygoma, destroying the sight of both eyes. The scar of entrance of the ball cannot be detected, but that of exit is evident; there was considerable hemorrhage from the wound.

June 11th. The globes of the eyes are collapsed, and the humours escaped; he has frequently very severe pain in the head, and cannot stand exposure to the sun, or excitement of any kind.

June 24th. Invalided.

64th Regt.—Private Michael Kirwan, wounded August 5, 1857, in Oude, with General Havelock's force, by a piece of shell which struck him on the right side of the head, producing total loss of vision of right eye. The eyeball is collapsed, but the lids remain; the left appears as if threatened with amaurosis from nervous influence, owing to the injury of the right eye; during the slightest exercise or exposure to the sun, he suffers from giddiness and dimness of vision, which compels him to remain quiet. Remains undisposed of.

[a] The cases of Lyons and Porter are mentioned by Assistant-Surgeon Chaumont, 1st Battalion of Rifles, in the Edinburgh Monthly Journal for December, 1858.

90th Regt.—Thomas Gallagher, wounded at Lucknow, November 16, 1857, by a musket-ball, which entered in front of the right ear, and passed out under the eye of the same side, close to the nose. One piece of bone came away from the entrance of the ball.

July 13th. Wound healed; cannot open his mouth to any extent, and has lost the sight of the right eye; the pupil of left is very much dilated, and the eye has an amaurotic appearance, but the ball of the eye is uninjured.

Invalided August 5th.

60th Regt.—Corporal John Jackson, wounded at Delhi, August 2, 1857, by a musket-ball in right eye, which took an unascertained course; there was not much loss of blood, and he was for about five weeks in nearly an unconscious state.

July 20th. Has lost the use of right eye, the humours having escaped; lids not much injured; has occasional headach, and has lost the sense of smell; is otherwise in good health. Was supplied with a glass eye.

July 21st, 1858. Duty.

DIVISION 4.— *With Fracture of the Lower Jaw.*

It is worthy of remark, the frequency of ununited fracture of the lower jaw in these cases of gunshot injury.

This bone is well supplied with blood, so that necrosis to any great extent does not generally follow severe comminution; still, callus is not thrown out so copiously for the repair of fracture as in the long bones of the extremities. Ununited fracture of the lower jaw does not seem to have been of such frequent occurrence amongst the wounded from the Crimea as those from India.

6 were admitted from India with fracture of the lower jaw. Of these, 3 were invalided; two sent to duty, and one to modified duty. Of these 6 cases, three were instances where the fracture still remained ununited, although the fractured ends of the bone were in contact. In one case the ball struck one side of the lower jaw, and was cut out on the opposite side, one month after, fracturing the bone on both sides. In one the ball was cut out from below the tongue. In one case, from a shell wound, there was a double fracture; one on the right side of ramus, and also another, near the symphysis, with great laceration of soft parts and deformity resulting; the first-named fracture remained ununited. In another case there was a double fracture from a musket-ball; the fracture at the entrance of the ball still remains ununited; that at exit has become united. In one case, from round-shot,

the whole of the left ramus of the lower jaw had been extracted at the time, or came away by exfoliation, leaving a large chasm and great deformity on this side of the cheek from laceration of the soft parts. In one case there was a fracture on the left side at the angle of the jaw still ununited.

Attempts were made to excite action in the ends of the bone by forcible rubbing together, and afterwards keeping the two fractured ends at rest by wire round the teeth, and a piece of cork placed between the teeth of the posterior fragment and that of the upper jaw, but without success. It was not thought advisable to try the effects of a seton or other means of inducing the effusion of new bone.

93rd Regt.—Private William Jeffreyes, wounded at Cawnpore, December 1, 1857, by a piece of shell on the right side of the body of the lower jaw. The soft parts were much torn, and the lower edge of the body of the bone was broken to pieces. There was also a vertical fracture of the bone near the symphysis.

July 12th. The first-named fracture is still ununited, and quite movable, and there is a large scar on the chin, opposite to it. There does not appear to be any necrosed pieces of bone coming away; the second fracture has united.

Invalided August 15, 1858.

8th Regt.—Private Edward Sweeny, aged 26, wounded at Delhi, September 14, 1857, by a musket-ball, which entered at the left side of the face, fracturing the lower jaw opposite to the first molar tooth, and passed across to a corresponding part on the opposite side of the lower jaw, where it made its exit. The portion of the symphysis of the lower jaw in front was for about three months quite loose and detached; several pieces of bone came away from the fracture on the left side; none came away from that on the right side, which became united in about three months after.

August 2nd. The fracture on the left side of the lower jaw still remains ununited, and quite movable, but there is no discharge from it; he cannot open his mouth, and his chin is distorted.

August 16th. Invalided.

20th Regt.—Enoch Pinder, aged 22, wounded at Sultanpore, February 23, 1858, by a round-shot on the left side of the lower jaw, fracturing this bone; nearly the whole of the left ramus of the lower jaw had been extracted at the time, or came away by exfoliation; the left shoulder-joint was also wounded by the firelock.

September 26th. Wound still discharging from a small

sinus, and there is a large cicatrix on this side of the face, which shows a deep hollow from the loss of bone. A dentist has made an artificial appliance, with several teeth attached, which fills up the deficient space in the left side of the jaw, and the patient feels considerable advantage from it.

November 3rd. Invalided.

23rd Regt.—Private James Morgan, wounded at Lucknow, March 16, 1858, by a musket-ball, which fractured the left ramus of the lower jaw at its angle; where the ball was extracted, several large pieces of bone have come away.

September 26th. Wounds healed; fracture still ununited.

September 27th. Duty.

CLASS III.—GUNSHOT WOUNDS OF THE NECK.

DIVISION 1.—*Simple Flesh Wounds and Contusions.*

7 cases were admitted, and 6 were discharged to duty. In one the ball entered close to the thyroid cartilage on the left side, and still remains in, but its position could not be ascertained with certainty. One was a flesh wound on the right of the larynx; ball dropped out. In another case the ball entered external to the right sterno-mastoid, and passed out at the margin of the trapezius, without injuring an important vessel or nerve.

It is remarkable that the large arteries and veins in the neck should escape injury so frequently in gunshot wounds, This may, in some measure, be accounted for by the structures in this region being so loose and movable that they yield or recede before any projectile.

78th Regt.—Private Benjamin Ritchie, wounded at Lucknow, September 25, 1857, by a musket-ball, in the left side of the neck, close to the thyroid cartilage; the ball still remains in, but its position cannot be ascertained with certainty. He spat up blood for some time after

June 11th. He cannot move his head except to a small extent laterally, and keeps his head bent down upon the chest. In consequence of this constrained position, the spinous processes of the fifth and sixth cervical vertebræ project.

June 17th. At Fort Pitt, under the supposition that the ball might possibly be lying embedded in this process, an incision was made downwards to the spinous processes, but no metallic substance could be detected.

August 30, 1858. Duty.

Class IV.—Gunshot Wounds of the Chest.

Division 1.—*Simple Flesh Contusions and Wounds.*

5 were admitted, and discharged to duty.

Division 2.—*With Injury of bony or cartilaginous Parietes, without Lesion of Contents.*

3 were admitted: one was a case of wound by a musket-ball, which struck the ribs on the right side, five inches below the nipple, and passed out a little to the posterior of the entrance. He spat up blood at the time, and frequently afterwards; several pieces of necrosed bone came away from both wounds. He was sent to duty.

The second was a case of wound by a musket-ball in the left breast, injuring the rib; several pieces of bone came away. He was invalided in consequence of impaired breathing.

Division 3.—*With Lesion of Contents by Contusion, or with Non-penetrating Wound.*

Two were admitted: one man was wounded by a round shot in the right breast which fractured the three upper ribs; no external wound. Both were sent to duty.

Division 4.—*Penetrating, and Ball lodged or apparently lodged.*

None admitted.

Division 5.—*Perforating Contents.*

Nine perforating gunshot wounds of the chest arrived from India, of which 5 have been sent to duty; 1 to modified duty; 1 invalided; and 2 died. 7 were wounded on the right side of the chest, and 2 on the left; in 4 instances it is mentioned that air passed out of the wounds of the chest. 8 were wounded by musket-ball, and 1 by grape-shot.

In all these cases there can be little doubt of the lung having been wounded, with, perhaps, the exception of Knox and Farrell. It is also remarkable that so many as five had so far perfectly recovered as to be able to return to duty, and the lung to have been so completely restored that nothing abnormal could be detected, either by percussion or auscultation, along the course of the ball, although it is to be supposed inflammation of the lung and pleural cavity took place to a greater or less extent in all. It is, however, stated that pneumonia occurred only in four instances; in one case there was hernia of the lung.

Out of 106 cases of this description of wound that occurred in the Crimea from the 1st April, 1855, to the end of the war, 82 died, and 24 were invalided or transferred, but it is not stated how many returned to duty. There are, however, the cases of one officer and one soldier detailed of recovery from this injury, and where the lung had perfectly regained its normal functions, one (the officer) returned to duty.

The wounds in all these cases from India were healed, with the exception of three, viz., in that of Doyle, Knox, and Moore. The case of Greenfield is interesting as showing not only a wound of the lung, but also of the œsophagus, recovering and returning to duty.

The two cases which terminated fatally, viz., Doyle and Knox, particularly that of Doyle, is interesting, as furnishing an admirable illustration of a perforating gunshot wound through the lung, the track of the ball still remaining open and fistulous, and being lined by a distinct, firm, false membrane, having numerous bronchial tubes of moderate size entering it; it also shows gangrene taking place in the healthy lung, and the wounded one remaining almost perfectly free from disease.

It is stated in the Report on the Wounded from the Crimea, vol. ii., page 321:—"Occasionally small circumscribed collections of pus took place in the track of the ball, surrounded and cut off from the remainder of the lung by consolidated pulmonary tissue, but in no case did the wounds of the organs remain a fistulous passage."

Private Walter Knox died at Gravesend of phthisis, and an extensive abscess was found extending from the wound near the right nipple to the crest of the ilium, with protrusion of the fractured ends of the ribs. The medical officer who made the post-mortem examination states that there was no communication between the cavity of the thorax and the wound; and that there was no cicatrix nor trace of injury to the lung in the position of the wound. But it appears that as the fractured ends of the ribs and the points of the false ribs protruded from the wound, the pleura and lung itself could hardly have escaped injury. This case might, perhaps, have been more properly placed under Division 3, but, on account of the probable lesion of the lung by the fractured ribs, and also from the difficulty of tracing the course of the ball, the lung being studded with tubercles, &c., it was thought better to be classed under Division 5.

It is a point well worthy of remark, that although from the position of the apertures of entrance and exit of the old round ball, it often appears as if it must have gone through the centre of the lung, still it will be found that the lung is only wounded superficially, or not through the thickest part, as is seen in the case of Doyle. This seems to be produced by the direction of the ball being deflected by striking the ribs, and then making its exit directly opposite. If a knife or piece of wire were put from one aperture to another, it would, in this case, pass directly through the thickest part of the lung. Preparations Nos. 3637, 3638, 3639, are from Private Owen Doyle.

A ball in passing through the substance of the lung destroys the life of the part, which suppurates, and either gradually heals, leaving a depressed cicatrix, usually, although not always, attached to the walls of the chest. During life, in many cases, it interferes so little with the respiratory murmur as not to be noticed by auscultation, as was very clearly observed in several of the cases from India. On other occasions the wound does not heal, nor the track of the ball close up, but remains open and fistulous, and becomes lined by a distinct membrane, as can be seen in preparation No. 3638. See Plate II., Fig. 1.

34th Regt.—Private George Bateman, aged 23, wounded at Cawnpore, November 30, 1857, by a musket-ball, which entered between the seventh and eighth ribs, immediately beneath the right axilla, passed inwards, downwards, and backwards, and made its exit between the eighth and ninth ribs posteriorly, about two inches from the spine. On admission he complained of great pain in the direction of the wound; there was considerable dyspnœa and cough, with bloody expectoration. On the 30th he had an attack of pneumonia.

December 17th. Was free from any bad symptoms.

July 13th. Wounds healed, percussion clear, and respiratory murmur distinct and clear all over the right side of the chest.

July 14, 1858. Duty.

93rd Regt.—David M'Kay, aged 25, wounded at Lucknow, November 16, 1857, by a musket-ball penetrating the right side of chest, emerging at the centre of the back, about an inch above the level of the lower angle of the scapula. During the progress of the case a piece of the spinous process came away; and during a full inspiration air came through the posterior wound with a loud report.

July 14th. Wound healed; respiration audible; pain in right side when lying down, otherwise quite well.

July, 1858. Duty.

60th Regt.—Private John Peake, aged 23, wounded at Delhi, September 14, 1857, by a musket-ball, which penetrated the body on the right side, about an inch from and in a line with the ensiform cartilage, wounding the organs within, and passing with slight obliquity downwards to the left side, to the ninth and tenth ribs, where it issued. and a piece of lung protruded; the wounds did not heal for five months; had vomiting of blood after the accident, and was insensible.

July 20, 1858. Wounds healed, and feels quite well; at the exit of ball there is a small nipple-like swelling protruding between the ribs, probably a portion of consolidated lung.

July 22nd. Invalided.

75th Regt.—Private Charles Greenfield, aged 25, wounded at Delhi, June 15, 1857, by a grape-shot, weight four ounces, on the left side of the chest. The ball entered through the anterior fold of the axilla, and passed downwards, backwards, and inwards, in a slanting direction, through the left lung, and made its exit apparently between the ninth and tenth ribs, close to the spinous process of the tenth vertebra. The entrance aperture soon healed; that of exit did not heal for seven months, and for six or seven days portions of his food passed through it, and air from the lung.

April 12, 1858. The external wounds have healed, but he suffers much from pain in the side, with a little cough, and much purulent expectoration. On examination there is dulness on percussion, and occasionally moist râles, but these have existed for some time, and are gradually diminishing. The pain is evidently muscular, and has been treated as such with relief.

27th. On examining his lung there is still at the spot above noticed the same dulness on percussion, with harsh respiration and increase of the vocal resonance. He is free from cough, and the position of the physical signs just mentioned corresponds with the course of the shot through his lung; their disappearance cannot for the present be looked for.

30th. Had an attack of pneumonia of the lower lobe of the left lung, with cough, and rust-coloured sputa.

June 1st. He vomited from the effects of antimony which he was taking. This is worthy of notice, on account of the œsophagus having been wounded.

2nd. A few moist râles could be heard.

5th. Quite well.

July 20th. Wounds healed; complains of some difficulty of breathing.

August 26, 1858. Modified duty.

Private Owen Doyle, aged 24; total service, $4\frac{5}{12}$ years, of which he was four months in Malta, one year in the Crimea, and the remainder in India. Wounded at Cawnpore, November 26, 1857, by a musket-ball, which entered the right side of the chest four inches to the outer side of right nipple, between the sixth and seventh ribs, about two inches under the right axilla, and passed inwards and backwards between the tenth and eleventh ribs posteriorly, where it lodged under the skin and muscles about two inches from the spinous processes of the vertebræ, where it was cut down upon and removed. The ball, on entering the chest, fractured the seventh rib, and on making its exit fractured the tenth rib. The usual symptoms attendant upon wounds of the lungs presented themselves. The man stated that air passed out of both wounds, and he spat up blood for a long time after. Soon after the wound he was attacked with pneumonia of the wounded lung, and for many days he suffered considerably. Ultimately all symptoms of this disease subsided. The wound healed, though he still suffered from cough, dyspnœa, and slight pain in the right side of the chest[a].

August 16, 1858. Admitted into Fort Pitt Hospital from India; wounds healed; complains of cough and shortness of breath. There was nothing abnormal to be detected in the right lung, or along the supposed track of the ball.

18th. Discharged to St. Mary's Barracks, to await invaliding documents.

31st. Readmitted, complaining of pain in the chest generally, but more especially over the left side of the chest, and also slightly over the seat of the old wound; respiration hurried; expectoration abundant and muco-purulent; percussion clear over the right side of the chest; vocal resonance in the inferior lobe of right lung, and along the track of the ball; dulness on percussion in left subclavicular region; respiratory murmur diminished, and crepitation distinctly audible; pulse strong, 86, and respiration 44 in the minute; cough very severe. Was cupped and blistered, and antimonials administered.

September 8th. The exit wound opened, and several small pieces of bone were taken away; complained of great pain, especially in the left side of the chest; pulse 80; respiration 28 per minute; wound discharging freely; healthy pus and air escaped on expiration and on coughing.

9th. Felt very weak, and there was a very fœtid smell from his breath; expectoration very profuse and purulent, and of a disagreeable odour. These symptoms contined up to the 20th, when they began to improve, and he seemed somewhat better, and was able to get out of bed and go about, although still troubled with cough and purulent expectoration, and the discharge from the wound posteriorly had almost ceased.

[a] This case is noticed by Assistant Surgeon Chaumont, Rifles, in the Edinburgh Medical Journal for December, 1858.

27th. Was feverish; pulse high; tongue coated; had a persistent pain in the left subclavicular region, and could not expectorate so freely as before. The fœtor of his breath and sputa returned as bad as ever, and the matter expectorated was of a thick, dark, stringy character. There was dulness on percussion over the whole of the left side of the chest. On the right side of the chest the percussion was clear, with only a few mucous râles, but the patient was in too exhausted a state to be accurately examined.

All these symptoms continued much the same, and he gradually became weaker, and on the 9th October the discharge from the wound still remained very profuse and fœtid, and air escaped very freely from it on coughing. He gradually sank, and died on the 15th October, 1848, eleven months after the wound.

Sectio Cadaveris, twenty hours after death.—*External appearances*. Body stout and well-formed; rigor mortis not passed away; muscles generally firm, and of the usual healthy appearance. There is a cicatrix on the right side of the chest, four inches below and to the outer side of the right nipple, and there is a small depressed aperture on the posterior part of the right side of the chest, about two inches from the spinous processes of the vertebræ, the integument around which is of a livid colour. *Cranium*. About one ounce of fluid at the base of the brain; slight subarachnoid effusion; the veins of pia mater congested; structure was otherwise healthy; weight 3 lbs. 5 oz. *Thorax*. The usual amount of serum in the pericardium; a fibrinous coagulum, not softened, in the right ventricle; the left side of the heart empty; structure of heart healthy; weight 12 oz. The *right lung* adhered firmly and universally to the walls of the chest by adhesions of old standing, more loosely along the anterior margin of the lung than posteriorly; structure of this lung perfectly healthy; crepitant, except a small portion of the inferior lobe close to the track of the ball, which will be more fully described afterwards. The left-bronchus having been tied, on introducing the nozzle of a pair of bellows into the trachea, the right lung was found to expand perfectly, and air to rush out externally at the posterior aperture, or that of exit of the ball, showing that there was a free communication between the trachea and the wound in the chest. The aperture of entrance of the ball was marked by a cicatrix four inches below and to the outer side of the right nipple, where it entered the thorax, between the sixth and seventh ribs, and seems to have passed backwards, and made its exit between the tenth and eleventh ribs, and where the ball, as stated in the

Fig. 1

3638

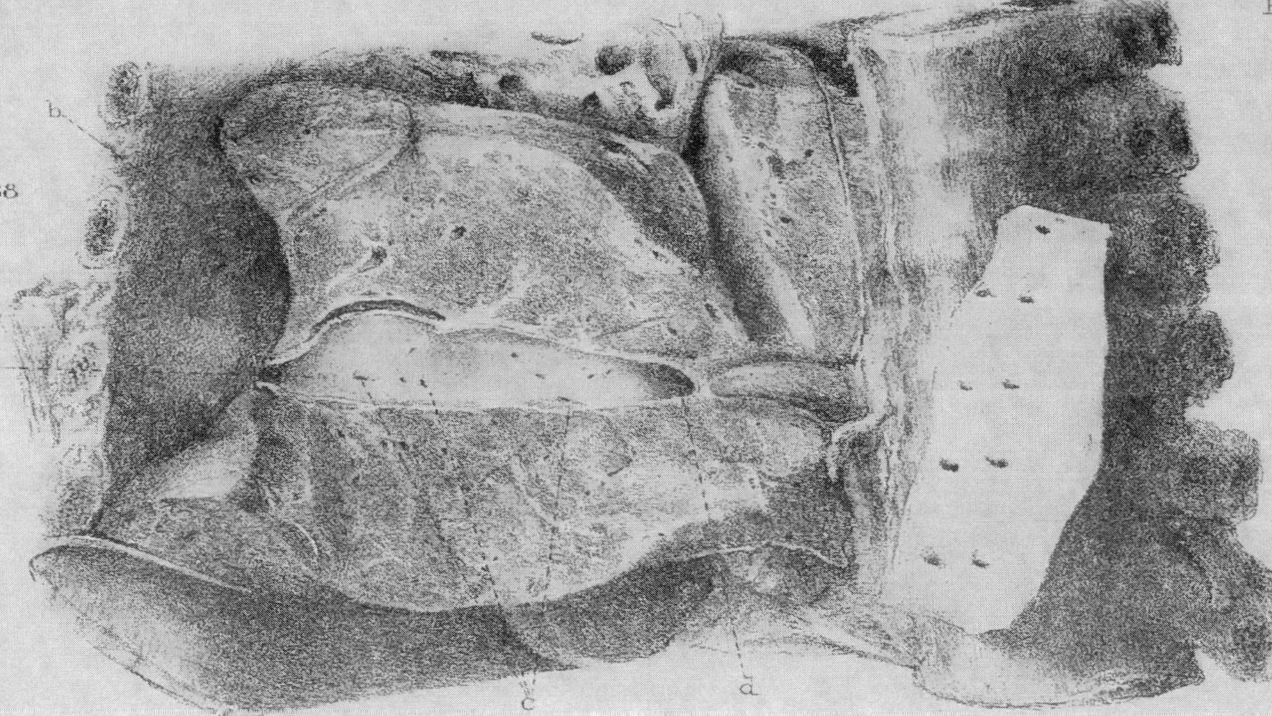

Fig. 2

3637

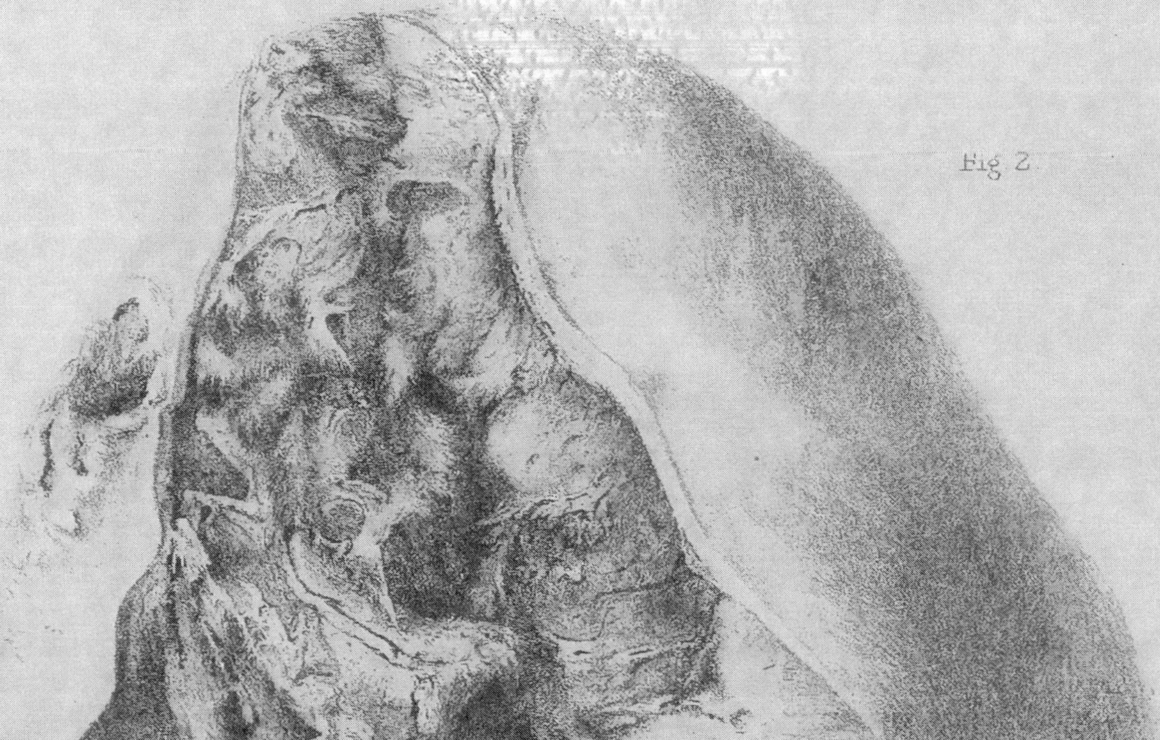

G.H.Ford. Fig 1. a. Track of ball. b. Lining membrane. c Bronchial tubes. d Unhealed exit of ball. W.West imp.

Fig 2. Gangrene of lung

report, was cut down upon and removed soon after being wounded. On introducing a probe through the posterior or the exit aperture, it was found to proceed for one inch in the muscular substance external to the thorax, and then to enter the pleura, and to wound the lung superficially. From this a sinus extends for three inches forwards in the substance of the lung to the entrance aperture, now closed. This sinus is larger than a common quill, and is lined by a distinct membrane with bronchial tubes opening into it. The lung seems to have recovered from the previous attacks of inflammation, except along the track of the ball, and where the bone had become necrosed, and kept the posterior wound open and discharging. The fractured ribs are united, and are not much displaced; that at the entrance of the ball projects somewhat inwards, and must have produced considerable irritation to the pleura and lung. See Plate II., Fig. 1, No. 3638. Numerous pieces of necrosed bone were found in a paper under the patient's pillow after his death, which were supposed to have come from the ribs. The upper half of the *left lung* adhered to the walls of the chest by old adhesions; inferior lobe adhered to the thoracic parietes by lymph of a more recent date, a coating of which fringed it, and covered its lower margin; structure of the upper half of the superior lobe entirely destroyed and broken up, forming a large, irregular cavity, filled with a dark, fœtid fluid, having several of the larger bronchial tubes intersecting it, the whole in a state of gangrene; inferior half of the same lobe in a state of gray hepatization, as also the upper half of inferior lobe, which was condensed, and sank in water. See Plate II., Fig. 2, No. 3637. The remainder of this lobe was œdematous, but otherwise free from disease. *Abdomen.*—Liver healthy; gall-bladder filled with dark bile; weight of liver, 3 lbs. 8 oz.; spleen healthy; weight, 11 oz.; kidneys healthy; weight of right, 8 oz.; left, 8½ oz.; stomach and intestines healthy; bladder empty and contracted; veins, as far as they could be traced, were found healthy, and the larger veins filled with dark coagula, and at parts fluid blood; but no fibrinous clots softened in their centres, nor pus globules, were detected. All the joints were healthy. This was at first thought to be a case of pyemia, where the pus globules or blood poisoning had excited inflammation in the left lung, resulting in pneumonia and gangrene; but, as stated above, none of the other morbid appearances usually found in cases of pyemia could be discovered..

Our knowledge of all the circumstances connected with, and the pathological appearances resulting from, poisoning of the blood in cases of open gunshot wounds, is not yet complete, so that this case, on more minute information on the subject, may be classed under the head of death from pyemia, or perhaps it is to be attributed to an accidental attack of pneumonia unconnected with the wound altogether. It is also remarkable that the inflammation should have attacked the sound lung, and not the one already in a state of disease.

In whatever manner the fatal result is to be explained, there can be little doubt that the wound in the chest influenced, in a most serious and baneful manner, the last fatal attack of pneumonia terminating in gangrene of the lung[a].

78th Regt.—Private Walter Knox, wounded at Lucknow, October 29, 1857, by a musket-ball, which struck him on the right side of the chest, near the nipple; the wound sloughed, and some pieces of bone exfoliated, leaving the respiration much impaired. The man stated that he was struck by a portion of shell, and that for three days after receiving the wound he expectorated blood. He was admitted into hospital at Gravesend from the ship "Argo" in the last stage of debility. A large abscess had formed, extending from the nipple to nearly the crest of the ilium, with numerous openings, through some of which the fractured ends of the broken ribs and the points of the false ribs protruded. On the post-mortem examination it was found that there was no cicatrix or trace of injury to the lung in the position of the wound, but that the lower and posterior portions of the right lung were a mass of disease, studded with tubercles in different stages, with several cavities, varying from the size of an acorn downwards. There was no communication between the cavity of the thorax and the wound, nor with the abdomen; but the peritoneum was generally much thickened with adhesions, and that portion corresponding with the seat of the abscess was almost of a cartilaginous texture, and divided by the knife with much difficulty. *Body* reduced to nearly a skeleton; the wound with the sinuses extended from the nipple to the crest of the ilium; the ribs on either side were detached from the lower portion of the sternum, and on the right side the fractured ends and also the points of the false ribs protruded through the skin. *Heart* large; pericardium contained about half an ounce of greenish, straw-coloured fluid; liver healthy; the gall-bladder was loaded with bile; intestines healthy

14th Light Dragoons.—Private John O'Neill, aged twenty-

[a] It is to be regretted that there is no record of the early treatment in these cases of perforating gun-shot wounds of the thorax, as to whether venesection was prevalent to a great, or only to a moderate extent. Still, I am inclined to think that it was not resorted to. In the case of O'Neill no venesection was employed.

nine years, wounded November 23, 1857, at Mundesand in the Deccan, by a musket-ball in the right side of the chest; the ball entered posteriorly at the inferior angle of the scapula, five inches above the spinous processes of the vertebræ, apparently between the eighth and ninth ribs, and was cut out immediately after from the right nipple. It had broken a rib at its exit. He went some distance on his horse from the field, and bled considerably; at the time his respiration was almost gasping, his countenance anxious, and pulse very feeble. He was almost in a state of collapse, and was thought to be dying. He was kept at perfect rest, his chest bandaged, and opium administered; for some days this treatment was continued; he was fed on barley-water; the pulse became rapid, and breathing painful; tongue dry and brown; thirst always urgent. On the 28th the wound began to discharge healthy pus; he had no cough, nor did he expectorate blood. The skin became cooler, and tongue began to clean, though the pulse continued frequent; the bowels had not been relieved since the wound had been received.

November 30th. 1 oz. of castor-oil relieved the bowels, and he was carried a march in a dooley, and took light puddings, milk, &c. On the 4th December, 3 oz. of port wine; no medicine. On the 9th could sit up for a few minutes to have his wounds dressed; they were both closing. The ends of the fractured ribs could be plainly felt; he was now allowed a little chicken diet. On the 15th the wound in the nipple had healed; he had gained strength, although he was very much prostrated. The chest did not act much on the right side during inspiration. On the 20th he could walk a little about the hospital; the posterior wound had nearly closed; there was slight crepitation about the lung near the wound, readily heard by the stethoscope; tongue had become quite clean; appetite good, and pulse natural. The chest was tender on pressure over the track of the ball, and he could not exert himself without a dull pricking pain there. The right side of the chest still acted very imperfectly. On the 5th September the wounds healed; respiration at entrance and exit of ball, and along supposed track through the lung, normal; and percussion clear.

September 8, 1858. Duty.

90th Regt.—Patrick Farrell, aged 24, wounded November 17, 1857, at Lucknow, by a musket-ball in the right side of the chest; the ball entered over the angle of the ninth rib of the right side, and passed out half an inch from the spinous process of last dorsal vertebra; several pieces of bone came away from the aperture of exit; he spat up blood at the time, and also on

D

several occasions afterwards. On the 10th October the wounds healed. It is difficult to say whether the internal organs were wounded or not, and if so, whether it was the lung or liver; respiratory murmur and percussion on this side normal.

October 15, 1858. Duty.

Private William Moore, aged 37, wounded at Cawnpore, November 28, 1857, by a musket-ball which penetrated the left side of the chest, three inches below and a little to the left of the nipple, and came out at a corresponding point behind where it injured the rib. The man states that wind came out of the wound, and that he spat blood.

July 13th. The anterior wound is healed; the posterior is still discharging, and a piece of diseased bone can be felt.

September 30, 1858. Duty.

Gunshot Wounds of the Diaphragm.

In the Report on the Medical and Surgical History of the British Army in the Crimea, vol. ii., page 317, it is stated that "it occasionally happened that both chest and belly had been wounded." One case is detailed, that of Dolan; and another is mentioned to have occurred in the 4th regiment. The first died on the tenth day, and the other sixteen hours after being wounded; but no case is recorded where a hernia of the abdominal organs had taken place into the pleural cavity. There appears to be a doubt as to whether Corporal Burke, 18th Regiment, was a case of rupture of the diaphragm without an external wound.

In the case of Greenfield, from India, there is every reason to suppose that the diaphragm was wounded on the *left* side, as the wound into the chest was so low that it was difficult to say whether the food passed out from the œsophagus or from the stomach just at its entrance. In Private Falloon's case it is probable that there was a wound of the diaphragm on the right side.

When the diaphragm is wounded, the floating viscera of the abdomen sometimes pass into the pleural cavity, and Mr. Guthrie is of opinion "these wounds never heal, but remain open ever after. When the diaphragm is wounded in the neighbourhood of the liver or spleen, adhesions may take place so as to prevent hernial protrusion."

It is always worthy of note, whether the wound is on the left or the right side, as to the probability of a hernia occurring, this being more liable to take place on the left than the right side.

There are three specimens of this rare and interesting description of wound in the Museum. In one case the soldier lived twenty-two years after, and did his duty; another lived one year, also in good health; and of the third there is no record.

No. 1260. Diaphragmatic hernia; the greater part of the transverse arch of the colon with the omentum are situated above the diaphragm, and in the left pleural cavity. The opening is in the muscular portion of the diaphragm, and about an inch in diameter.

No. 1268. Displays the whole of the stomach and greater part of the transverse arch of the colon (both rather small) with the omentum situated in the lower and anterior part of the left cavity of the thorax. The anterior surface of the stomach is firmly attached to the lower lobe of the lung; the lung at this side, as may be expected, has become much reduced in size, and occupies the superior and posterior part of its proper cavity. The right lung is smaller than the left, and from the circumstance of the heart being much displaced by the stomach and colon, and instead of extending across from the second rib of the right side to the sixth of the left, as this viscus naturally does, it now lies nearly parallel to the spine, having the apex almost on a level with the coronary ligament of the liver, and, being of a natural size, must have proved much less yielding during inspiration than the stomach and the colon on the other side of the chest.

The opening in the diaphragm extends in a transverse direction near to the centre of the dorsal attachment of the left side of this muscle, and the objects forming the hernia have contracted adhesions with the diaphragm and other parts, and the peritoneum lining the former is in many places continuous with that covering the colon.

This very interesting specimen was taken from the body of Sergeant Denis Barry, 88th Regiment, who died on the 4th January, 1833, in consequence of gangrene of the left lower extremity, produced, as it was supposed, by metastasis of a severe rheumatic affection of the larger joints. He was wounded at Fuentes D'Onores, in 1811, in the left breast; death took place twenty-two years after the wound. After receiving the wound he had never been able to wear his knapsack with ease, and his breathing became much affected whenever he walked quickly or ascended a hill.

No. 1269. Diaphragmatic hernia, the result of a gunshot wound. The greater part of the stomach, the transverse arch of the colon, and omentum, are seen in the left pleural cavity. This lung adheres very firmly and closely to the walls of the chest, as low as the ninth ribs, by adhesions of long standing.

The lung is pushed to the upper half of the cavity, but, on account of adhesions to the ribs, it is compressed into a thin layer, which lines the walls of the thorax. The heart is also displaced, and lies behind and a little to the right of the sternum. The large curvature of the stomach lies in front, and first showed itself on opening the chest. The transverse arch of the colon is to the left of the stomach, and between it and the ribs. The stomach reaches a little higher in the chest than the gut. There is an opening in the diaphragm, with rounded margins, $2\frac{1}{2}$ inches in diameter, situated 2 inches to the left of the œsophagus; the peritoneum lining the diaphragm proceeds through the aperture, and is continuous with the pleura. Although the serous surface around the opening is smooth and uninterrupted, still there is some thickening and an appearance of old cicatrization. In the pleural sac close to the opening in the diaphragm, on its posterior and external margin, the stomach, colon, and omentum adhere firmly to the pleura, covering the diaphragm and ribs to the extent of a few inches. There are also two broad, thin, and loose bands of adhesion, about 8 inches in length, stretching from the omentum to the base of the pericardium. The stomach and colon are, however, loose and free in the pleural sac; the parts in the aperture of the diaphragm are free from adhesions, and not contracted, and the fingers were easily introduced through it, from the abdomen into the thorax. The œsophagus, after penetrating the diaphragm in the usual place, takes a sharp turn to the left side; the stomach then enters the thorax, a portion of the cardiac extremity of which still, however, lies in the abdomen, in front and to the right of the spleen; the larger part, having entered the chest, curves round and descends to the opening in the diaphragm. The pyloric orifice lies immediately in the aperture; about a foot and a half of the transverse arch of the colon, with the omentum attached, are also in this cavity. On the skin exactly opposite and corresponding to the diaphragm are two cicatrices in the left side of the chest, one situated between the eighth and ninth ribs, three and a half inches from their cartilages where the musket-ball had entered, and the other, its exit, between the eleventh and twelfth ribs, close to the transverse processes of the vertebræ. The ball, in its course through the thorax, must have wounded the diaphragm, and permitted the hernia of the stomach and colon. See Plate III.—*Donor, Dr. Williamson, Staff-Surgeon.*

31st Regt.—Private Thomas Fletcher, aged 40, an Irishman, a weaver, 5 feet $6\frac{1}{2}$ inches; stout and healthy frame. Total service, $20\frac{4}{12}$ years, of which $19\frac{5}{12}$ years were spent in India,

Pl. III.

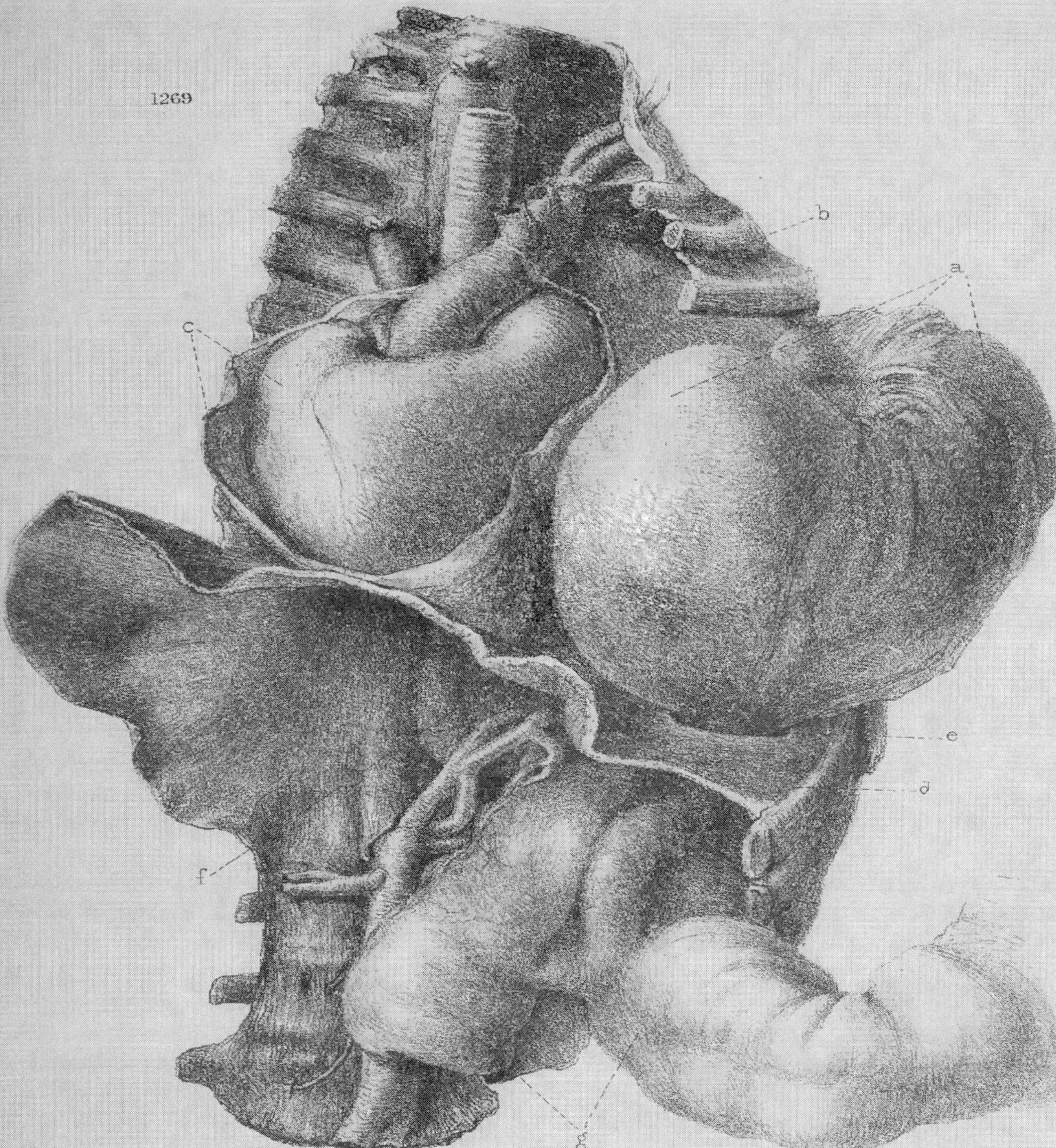

a. Stomach, Colon & Omentum in the left side of the Chest. b. Lung compressed. c. Heart &
ericardium. d. Diaphragm. e. Aperture in Diaphragm. f. Æsophagus & portion of Stomach. g. Small & large intestine.

G.H. Ford. W. West imp.

where he had two or three attacks of intermittent fever. He was wounded at Sobraon, February 10, 1846, by a musket-ball in the left side of the thorax, entering between the eighth and ninth ribs, and about four inches from their cartilages, and making its exit close to the transverse process of the eleventh dorsal vertebra, and between the eleventh and twelfth ribs.

He landed in England on the 13th January, 1847, in good general health. Admitted into Fort Pitt General Hospital on the 20th January, under observation for the wound in his side. Discharged well on the 2nd February. On the 11th February, immediately after his dinner, he was attacked with vomiting and pain in the left side over the spleen; this continued until the evening of the 12th, when he was admitted into this hospital. He could not account for his sickness; he had been quite well in the morning, and his bowels had been acted on.

On admission his skin was cold, pulse quick, small, and wiry, 90; respiration natural; pain over the spleen increased on pressure. On the 13th the pain had left the side and shifted to the shoulder and clavicle. It was not acute. He was free from all other pain and all inflammatory symptoms to the hour of his death, neither was there any pain on pressure in the region of the stomach, nor any tension of the belly, but, on the contrary, an extraordinary hollowness, or drawing in about the umbilicus, resembling very much in appearance a man suffering from "Asiatic cholera."

His bowels could not be acted on, and the irritability of his stomach and vomiting of all things swallowed continued to the last. He began to sink in the afternoon of the 16th, gradually became weaker, and died on the 18th February, it being eight days from the time he was first attacked with vomiting, and twelve months from the time he was wounded.

The treatment consisted first of an emetic, with a blister over the spleen. Afterwards full doses of calomel and opium, morphia, and hydrocyanic acid, frequently repeated, castor-oil combined with croton-oil, both by the mouth and injections, turpentine injections and fomentations to the abdomen, hot baths, and hot bottles to his feet, and beef-tea injections, were the remedies administered.

Post-mortem Examination thirty hours after death.—*External Appearances.* Body stout and well formed; skin shrivelled, more particularly that of the hands and feet; features contracted and indicative of a person having died under great suffering; muscles rigid. *Cranium.* About one ounce of fluid at the base of the brain; veins of the pia mater congested, as also those of the velum interpositum and choroid plexuses; section of the brain presented many bloody points; weight of brain, 3 lbs. *Thorax.* The structure of both lungs was healthy; the posterior part of the right was attached to the chest by adhesions of long standing; the heart was of its natural size, and its structure healthy. *Abdomen.* On tracing the small intestines, five intussusceptions were found, the first situated a foot and a half from the duodenum, and the other four were generally from eight to ten inches apart. The portion intus-suscepted was in each about two inches; there was no vascularity or congestions in the intussusceptions, or in any of the abdominal viscera. Both portions of the stomach, viz., the part in the chest and the part in the abdomen, contained a quantity of dark fluid, mixed with portions of food and medicine. The duodenum and upper part of the jejunum, as far as the first intus-susception, was distended with flatus; the small intestines below the invagination although not distended, but in their normal condition, were coated with mucus tinged with bile. The caput cæcum and ascending colon, to where it entered the chest, were distended, and contained a quantity of fluid and hardened fæces.

The transverse arch of the colon was distended with flatus and some feculent matter; the descending colon and rectum were empty; liver healthy, weight, 4 lbs. 4 oz., kidneys healthy, weight of right, 6 oz., left, 6 oz. 2 dwts.

Remarks.—Fletcher was in perfect health until immediately after he had taken a full meal, which, no doubt, he had frequently done since the time he had received the wound. It may, therefore, be asked what was the immediate cause of vomiting, and the sudden attack of illness; probably, the portion of the stomach still in the abdomen having become over-distended, spasmodic contraction of the diaphragm may have been induced, and prevented the food from entering the larger portion of the stomach, situated in the thorax, but it might have been supposed that after the contents of the lower portion had been ejected, irritability of this organ would have ceased, which did not take place, but continued to the last without the slightest alleviation.

The reason for supposing it was spasmodic contraction of the diaphragm is, that on examination the opening in this muscle was found large enough to admit two fingers with ease along the side of the gut.

Although it was, however, known that he had been wounded in the side, yet it was never suspected that the wound was in any way connected with the disease for which he was under treatment; his general appearance was most peculiar, the contracted state of the abdomen, the total absence of all pain in his belly after the first day, and of all inflammatory symptoms, and the occurrence of pain in his left shoulder. It is known that in diseases of the liver pain in the right shoulder is a common symptom. The pain in Fletcher may have had the same origin, whatever that may be, as no satisfactory explanation has as yet been given of it, except that it may depend upon some irritation of the ramifications of the phrenic nerve communicated along its course to its origin from the cervical and bronchial plexus, and then reflected by twigs distributed to the shoulder. A number of the symptoms which presented themselves in this case were those usually attendant on strangulated inguinal hernia, viz., incessant vomiting and obstinate constipation, pulse small and wiry; but there was no stercoraceous vomiting, dissection showing that it could not occur.

The intus-susceptions were the first morbid appearances seen on opening the body, and the remark was immediately made that they did not present the appearance of invaginations which are the cause of death, but rather what are seen to take place during the latter stages of life when a patient has no symptoms of derangement of the intestinal canal. It is, therefore, probable that the intus-susception took place after the commencement of the fatal disease, and was not the cause of it, but to be attributed to the violent peristaltic motions excited by the action of the croton-oil which was administered.

At the first view of the case it appeared to throw some light on the physiology of vomiting, as to how far the muscles of the abdomen and diaphragm co-operate with the stomach in this mechanical act. But the whole of the stomach not being displaced into the thorax, whatever influence they possess may have been, therefore, exercised on the part in the abdomen.

It is also to be supposed that the contents of the stomach, and transverse arch of the colon, situated in the thorax, remained the samé from the time they became strangulated.

Mr. Guthrie's remarks as to wounds of the diaphragm never uniting may be the fact generally, but in a case where a wound of the diaphragm is small, and the patient is kept quiet and on proper diet, there appears to be no reason for supposing that the wound would not close; the base of the lung might adhere to the diaphragm, close up the opening, and so form a boundary between the thorax and abdomen, and thus prevent a hernial protrusion. Besides, it is only in those cases where a hernia has taken place that a surgeon, on an autopsy taking place, makes such a careful examination of those parts. I am therefore disposed to think that in some cases of wounds in the lower part of the thorax the diaphragm has been injured, and the patient has recovered from its effects so as never after to draw any attention to it; and that union of the divided fibres of the diaphragm or pleuritic adhesion have taken place in some cases, and prevented a hernia from forming, as is possibly the case in that of Greenfield and Eally, and others.

It is very remarkable that this extraordinary malposition of the stomach and colon should have produced so little inconvenience to the patient, and that in every respect Fletcher was in perfect health until strangulation took place.

The case of Sergeant Denis Barry, who was wounded in nearly the same situation, where there was also a hernia of the stomach and colon into the thorax, and continued to do his duty as a soldier for nearly twenty-two years, shows how little inconvenience he also experienced. Had the exact state of things been accurately diagnosed during life, what steps could have been taken for his relief? Would a surgeon be warranted in cutting into the abdomen and reducing the hernia?

In this case it would have been impossible, on account of adhesions of the displaced viscera to the surrounding parts. The diagnosis of such a displacement would be extremely difficult, if not impossible. There was, in January, 1847, under my care in this hospital a patient wounded in nearly the same situation, viz. :—

Private Thomas Eally, aged 25, was wounded on the 29th December, 1843, at Marajpore, by a grape-shot, which entered about three inches below and to the outer side of the left nipple, between the eighth and ninth ribs; it was cut out shortly after the accident, behind and at the angle of the eleventh rib. He suffered severely from pleuritis of the left side in 1844. His general health is now (January, 1847) good, and he has no complaint except shortness of breathing, or rather uneasiness in his chest when wearing his knapsack and cross-belts.

It is probable that the diaphragm was wounded in this case also; if so, the wound may possibly have closed, or pleuritic adhesions have formed and prevented a hernial protrusion. If, however, Eally was seized in the same manner as Fletcher, after all other means had failed, should operative measures be resorted to? I am disposed to think that few surgeons would be inclined to undertake such an operation from the great uncertainty as to the state of the parts that might exist.

GUNSHOT WOUNDS OF THE HEART AND GREAT VESSELS.

The Museum can only furnish three cases of these formidable wounds.

No. 173. Heart exhibiting a lance wound, which penetrated the right ventricle through the diaphragm. Death five months after the wound.—*Donor, Mr. Guthrie*—who remarks: "If this man had lived long enough, he might have furnished an instance of hernia of the stomach or intestines into the pericardium."

No. 174. A punctured wound of the right ventricle, close to the apex. Instant death.

No. 403. Abdominal aorta, showing a horizontal wound through its coats, caused by the point of a bayonet. Death three hours after.

Class V.—Gunshot Wounds of the Abdomen.

Division 1.—*Simple Flesh Contusions and Wounds.*

Four cases of simple flesh wounds arrived from India, and have been discharged to duty. In one case the ball is reported by the surgeon of his regiment to be lodged somewhere above Poupart's ligament; profuse hemorrhage followed, which stopped of itself. In another case the ball entered below the ensiform cartilages on the right side, and passed out at the extremity of the last floating rib on the right side. The third was a slight wound from grape-shot.

Division 2.—*Contusions and Non-penetrating Wounds.*

Two cases were admitted from India, and have been sent to duty.

64th Regt.—Private James Falloon[a], wounded at Cawnpore, November 28, 1857, by a musket-ball which entered two inches below the ensiform cartilage, on the right side, and at the margin of the cartilage of the false ribs, and passed downwards and backwards, and was cut out opposite the extremity of the last floating rib. He vomited florid blood, according to his own statement, at the time; there was no external bleeding. The ball passed behind the ribs, and there is little doubt that the peritoneum was slightly wounded, and probably the diaphragm.

August 18, 1858. Wound healed. Duty.

35th Regt.—Private John Lowe, aged 39, wounded January 25, 1857. The ball entered the abdomen on a line with the margins of the ribs, and near their angles; it was extracted shortly after through an incision made in the epigastric region, it having lodged beneath the skin in that locality; no discoloration of the integuments between the entrance of the ball

[a] Noticed by Assistant-Surgeon Chaumont, Rifle Brigade, in the Edinburgh Monthly Journal for December, 1858.

and where it was cut out was at any time perceptible to mark its course; he vomited blood at the time; had not any external bleeding; his wound healed in the usual period, and he was discharged from hospital six months after its receipt. He has since suffered much from pain and tenderness in the region of the epigastrium, and he has been unable to wear his accoutrements, the pressure causes so much suffering; under the circumstances, he is unfitted for the active duties of a soldier.

April 28th. Invalided.

DIVISION 3.—*Penetrating or perforating, with Lesion of the Intestine.*

Two were admitted from India, and both will be invalided,

It is well known that gunshot wounds of the solid viscera, as also those of the small intestines, are generally fatal; still, this is not invariably the case, as is seen by the very fine specimen, No. 1271. Wounds of the large intestines are also not so formidable or dangerous, especially when the wound is in the neighbourhood of the cæcum or sigmoid flexure, where the intestine is more fixed and bound down, and only partially covered by the peritoneum.

Two cases of abnormal anus by gunshot perforation appear to be a large proportion to the total wounded, 603. The 2296 cases of wounded from the Crimea furnish only one such case, Private James Beehan, 19th Regiment, who is now in Guy's Hospital, never having recovered from the wound, though it has occasionally closed and again re-opened, as has taken place in every one of the three cases now detailed. A note from Mr. Birkett, dated 21st January, 1859, says:—"He (Beehan) has since my last report suffered with severe attacks from albuminuria, and is anasarcous." For particulars of this case, *vide* page 330 of the Report on Crimean Wounded[a].

In the case from which preparation No. 1270 was taken, the wound is likewise on the left side, and the colon was wounded at a part where it is *entirely covered* by peritoneum. This makes the fifth case of wound of the large intestine detailed in this Report, and in that of the wounded from the Crimea.

It is worthy of remark that in all these five cases the artificial anus is on the left side, and almost precisely in the same situation, with the exception of the one, No. 1270. In Hogan there was a partial fracture of the ilium. In Beehan there was an injury of the vertebræ, and probably also of the kidney. In

[a] Since the above was written, this case has terminated fatally; and the post-mortem appearances, which have been kindly furnished by Mr. Birkett, will be found at page 111.

M'Cartney and Henderson there was no such complication. Private Henderson was under my care in 1844.

As already stated, all these five cases of wounds of the large intestines, and also the three of the diaphragm, are on the left side. This at first sight would lead to the supposition that the left side of the body was more exposed in action than the right, and might probably be accounted for, by soldiers placing the left side more forward when in the act of firing, supposing that the wounds were received when in this position. This appears, however, not to be the case, but is to be attributed to wounds of the right side of the abdomen being more fatal than those on the left, in consequence of the liver occupying so much space on that side; for on examining the wounds in the thorax received from India, out of 19 I find that 15 were wounded on the right, and only 4 on the left side.

The following three very interesting cases of gunshot wound of the sigmoid flexure of the colon are examples of this lesion.

32nd Regt.—Private Cornelius Hogan[a], aged 34, wounded June 30, 1857, at Lucknow, in the left hip, an inch and a half below the crest of the left ilium, and nearly midway between the anterior and superior spinous process of the ilium and the spinous process of the back. The ball entered and must have passed into or wounded the sigmoid flexure of the colon, and is supposed still to remain in, as it has never, as far as the man knows, been passed by stool. For twenty-two days he passed his fæces entirely through the opening, but since then he has never passed any feculent matter through the wound, but only flatus; this also has ceased for the last fortnight, but there is still a considerable discharge of purulent matter, and he complains of pain in the back.

He was transferred from Fort Pitt to Yarmouth Hospital, July 4, 1858, and from thence was sent to the depôt of his regiment, which he joined on October 28th.

He was tried by court martial on December 9th, and was sentenced to forty-two days' imprisonment at Fort Clarence, with such labour as the surgeon in charge considered him capable of performing without risk. Previous to appearing before the surgeon he had undergone an hour's shot drill, which caused the wound to reopen. He was consequently sent to the garrison hospital, and was transferred to Fort Pitt, January 29, 1859, with fæces still passing through the wound.

March 13, 1859. Wound healed, and he enjoys good health; but has been invalided as being unfit for further service.

[a] This case is noticed in the Edinburgh Monthly Journal for December, 1858, by Assistant Surgeon Chaumont.

10th Regt.—Private Michael M'Cartney, aged 27, wounded by a musket-ball, May 11, 1858, at Chitawarah, which passed through the left side of the body, from behind forwards, passing through the diameter of the colon. For a period of three months he passed fæces through the opening.

February 25, 1859. Wound still continues to discharge; complains of great pain in the abdomen; has piles, and is troubled with diarrhœa; he is rather anemic in appearance.

March 4th. Diarrhœa still continues; a truss has been applied over the fistulous opening.

10th. The truss discontinued, as it causes much flatulence.

15th. No improvement; complains of cold and shivering.

13th Regt.—Private John Henderson, aged 36, wounded at Cabul, in October, 1840, by a musket-ball which entered the left side at the extremity of the last rib, and made its exit about two inches from the spine, passing obliquely downwards and backwards, penetrating the colon, followed by very profuse discharge of fæces; the wound was of a very dangerous nature. He was taken prisoner, and suffered great privations. He was admitted into Fort Pitt, July, 1844, with both apertures of entrance and exit of ball discharging fæces. Various methods of treatment were tried to effect a cure, but without success; the wounds would close for a short time, and then break out again, so that he was eventually discharged the service, August 26, 1844.

The following preparation is from a sailor who was wounded in the act of rowing towards the enemy. It is to be regretted that there is no detailed history of this interesting case; but, from the state of parts now exhibited, there can be no doubt that the patient lived for some time, perhaps years, in a most wretched condition.

No. 1270. Gunshot wound of the large intestine, terminating in artificial anus. Vide Plate IV., Fig. 1.

The ball entered on the left side, wounded the colon as it is curving downwards to become the descending colon, and passed out, fracturing the eleventh rib at its anterior third. The aperture in the abdominal walls is about 3 inches in diameter, and a knuckle of intestine protrudes. The opening in the gut is about 1½ inches in diameter, and the mucous surface is everted and has become very firmly united to the integuments by adhesions of old standing. So much is this the case, that the mucous membrane and skin have become quite continuous, the intestine has also contracted firm adhesions to the adjacent peritoneum on the inner side.

A quill is inserted into the upper part of the gut, which is

Pl IV.

Fig. 1.

1270

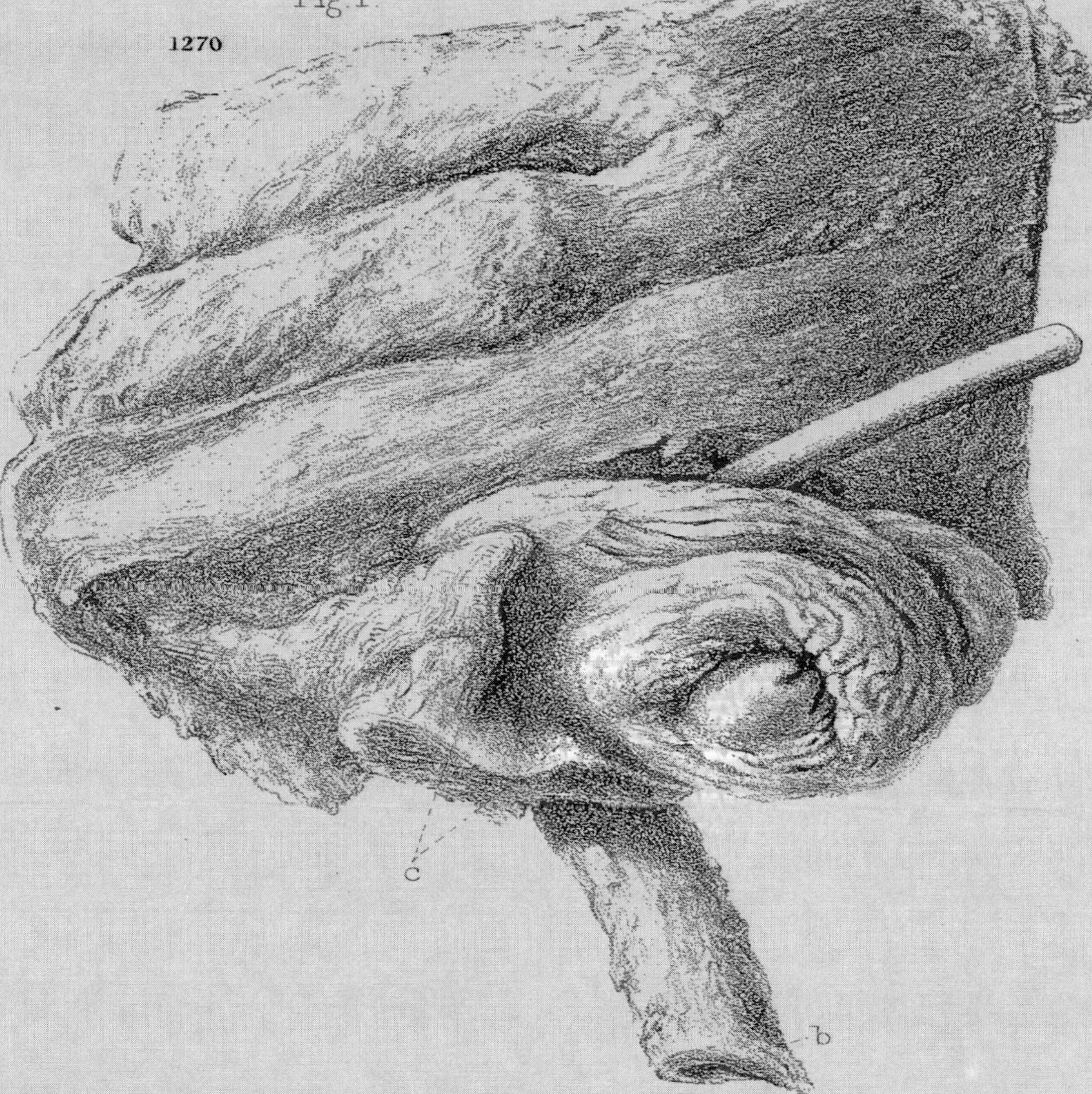

2004

Fig. 2.

Fig. 1. a. Probe in upper portion of intestine.
b. Lower portion of intestine, contracted.
c. Everted mucous membrane & integuments perfectly continuous.

Fig. 2. Piece of cane, drawn from the bladder, see p. 50.

W West imp.

Pl. V.

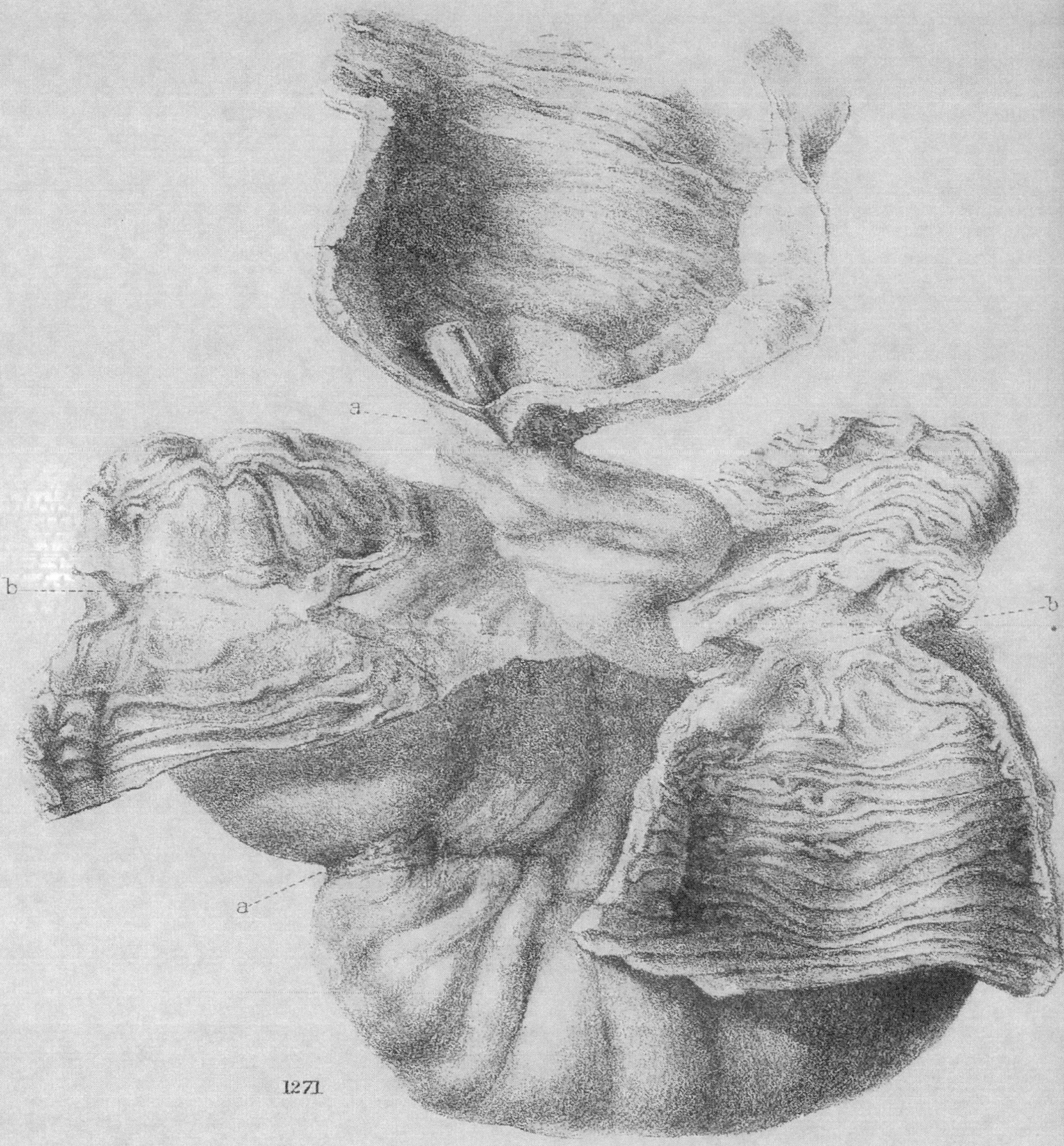

G. H. Ford. W. West imp.

a. Contractions;
b. Contractions laid open.

of the usual caliber, and the mucous membrane is healthy. The bowel below the wound is very much contracted from want of use, but pervious. The fæces were voided through the preternatural opening.

The following preparation of a perforating gunshot wound through several folds of the small intestine, followed by recovery, is, as far as I am aware, quite unique.

No. 1271. Two pieces of the small intestine; jejunum showing the results of injury by gunshot wound. The larger piece of intestine exhibits three constrictions of that gut, two of which have been laid open to show the interior, and the third one remains entire. In the inside these contractions present much the appearance of a cicatrix, being totally devoid of the normal villous character of mucous membrane of the intestine; above and below it is bounded by a sharp and well-defined line of the natural lining of the intestine. Externally these constricted points are covered by a layer of old granular lymph; they were of a darker hue and more vascular than other portions of the small intestine, which, however, presented throughout the arborescent vascularity and soddened state constantly observed in rapidly fatal cases of blue spasmodic cholera. The smaller piece of intestine exhibits a fourth constriction of the gut, capable of admitting only a good-sized quill..—*Donor, J. R. Taylor, Surgeon, 80th Regiment.*

This preparation is from Private Paul Massey, 80th Regiment, who was shot in the abdomen at the battle of Ferozeshah, December 22, 1845. The symptoms consequent immediately upon the wound appear to have been so inconsiderable that it is recorded by Dr. Mac Donald (then surgeon of the regiment) that it was his opinion that the ball had coursed round the abdomen, and not penetrated or passed through that region. The patient, however, shortly before his death, stated he had passed blood by stool after the receipt of the injury. Recovery followed slowly, but appeared to be perfect. The soldier, however, became subject to attacks of bowel complaint, gradually becoming more frequent, and for the last twelve months of his life he was nearly constantly under treatment for symptoms of dysentery of the land scorbutic type. Whilst in hospital on account of this disease, he was seized, on the 13th May, 1851, with blue spasmodic cholera, terminating fatally the same day. Death five and a half years after being wounded.

Cholera was then prevalent in the neighbourhood, and became epidemic in the regiment in the following month.

Post-mortem Appearances, an hour and a half after Death.— Externally. Livid; but less so than during life; not much emaciated; cicatrix of a wound in left linea semilunaris, about four inches above the crista ilii, and on the same plane posteriorly, another cicatrix, an inch to the left of the spine.—*Head*. General livid appearance of meninges and cerebral substance, some milky opacity on the upper surfaces of the hemispheres, slight serous effusion under arachnoid.—*Thorax*. Adhesions on right side; lungs partially collapsed; structure healthy; heart normal; fluid blood in left ventricle.—*Abdomen*. Omentum firmly adherent to the internal surface of anterior cicatrix, and gathered into a knot at that point. The intestines neither there nor elsewhere morbidly adherent, but the fold of intestines immediately opposed to the cicatrix presented a line of contraction, as if a ligature had been tied round the gut. The fold of intestine immediately above presented the same appearance, and on the first fold, four inches from the first noticed contraction, and situated in a line below the umbilicus, was another similar appearance. The mucous surface of the small intestine generally was pale-pinkish in colour; no ulceration of large intestine; upper part of colon attenuated and contracted in situ; rectum thickened; stomach pale; liver small, congested; gall-bladder half filled with dark viscid bile; spleen small; kidneys healthy. See Plate V.

It is curious to remark, on post-mortem examination of a case of direct gunshot perforation of the abdomen, that the intestine is wounded in many places considerably removed from the direct course of the ball. Is this removal of wounded portions of intestine from the line of the ball due solely to the natural peristaltic action, or to something more than this, as the result of the injury? Probably the latter influence is considerable; as it has been remarked, and I believe truly, that under perforation of the intestines by ulceration there is not only contraction in caliber, but marked *shortening* of the intestinal canal. This action beyond the peristaltic may be expected, and really appears to follow equally perforations by injury and disease, thus explaining the withdrawal of the wounded points of intestine from the line of the ball, as indicated by the orifices of entrance and exit.

In a case that came under the observation of Deputy Inspector General T. Alexander, C.B., the small intestines were found to have been wounded sixteen times[a]; and in preparation 1272 the small intestines are perforated four times, and the mesentery twice.

No. 1272. Gunshot wound of the small intestines and me-

[a] Mr. Guthrie's Commentaries, p. 576.

sentery, the former wounded in three places, and the latter in one. Death twenty-four hours after the accident.

No. 1125. A gunshot wound of the large curvature of the stomach. The man lived eight hours after the accident.

Class VI.—Gunshot Wounds of the Back and Spine.

Division 1.—*Simple Flesh Contusions and Wounds.*

Three were admitted, and two were sent to duty.

Division 2.—*With Fracture of the Vertebræ, without Lesion of the Spinal Cord.*

Six have been admitted; two have been discharged to duty, two invalided, and two remain; all were the result of musket-balls; one was a case of fracture of the ilium and spinous process of the lumbar vertebræ, with the wounds still unhealed. One with fracture of the spinous process of the dorsal vertebræ; wounds still open.

Two cases of wounds of the sacrum; in one of them the wound was still open, and a probe could be passed right across from the one aperture to the other. The last was a wound of the spinous process of the lumbar vertebræ, also still unhealed.

The two following cases are examples of this description of wound.

93rd Regt.—Sergeant James Munro; wounded at Lucknow by a musket-ball through the loins; the ball entered a little behind and below the crest of the left ilium, and passed a little upwards and backwards, nearly across the back, and made its exit immediately above the crest of the right ilium; numerous pieces of bone came away from both apertures. Shortly after the injury the urine was tinged with blood, and it is doubtful whether the two last vertebræ are injured.

12th July. The aperture of exit of ball has closed; that of entrance is still open, and discharging, and the probe can be introduced for a considerable distance, but bare bone is not detected; he is unable to sit upright, and he has lost considerable power over the limbs; has incontinence of urine.

Invalided 29th September, 1858.

24th. Private Patrick Farrell, aged 30, wounded 7th July, 1857, by a musket-ball which entered on the right side of the third lumbar vertebra, two inches from the spinous processes passed across the back, and made its exit a little below the centre of the crest of the left ilium; several pieces of bone came away from the aperture of exit.

August 2nd. Aperture of entrance is healed; that of exit

is still discharging, leading down to diseased bone. There is some thickening over the spinous processes of the lumbar vertebræ. Undisposed of.

DIVISION 3.— *With Lesion of the Spinal Cord.*

None were admitted from India; but the following cases from preparations in the Museum illustrate this injury.

No. 2912. Dorsal portion of the spine, showing a bullet lodged in the canal. The ball appears to have entered exactly through the centre of the arch, which, with the spinous process, is partly broken away. From a sergeant of the 5th Dragoons, who was shot by a private of the regiment.

No. 2913. Is from Private R. Greive, 3rd Light Dragoons, who was wounded at Rhamnuggur, Nov. 21, 1849, by a musket-ball which entered below the right mamma, penetrated the lower lobe of the right lung and diaphragm, grazed the upper surface of the liver, and passed between the head of the eleventh rib and the vertebræ. It lodged in the spinal canal, and caused paraplegia. Death four days after the injury.

No. 2914. Fifth dorsal vertebra, exhibiting fracture of part of the right side of its arch by a pistol-ball which is lodged in the canal. The ball entered the right deltoid muscle and proceeded downwards on the outside and upper part of chest near to the spine, and finally lodged in the canal. The course of the ball was not known till the death of the patient, which took place thirty days after the injury. The body and limbs below the navel were deprived of sensation and motion; the urine required removal by the catheter, or dribbled away; and the fæces were passed involuntarily; followed by sloughing of the integuments of the sacrum and trochanters. From an officer who was wounded in a duel.

No. 2915 is a gunshot fracture of the atlas and axis. The ball dropped into the mouth, and the man died in thirty days after the wound.

CLASS VII. — GUNSHOT CONTUSIONS AND WOUNDS OF THE PERINEUM, AND GENITAL AND URINARY ORGANS, NOT BEING, AT THE SAME TIME, WOUNDS OF THE PERITONEUM.

Three very interesting cases have been admitted from India. In two very similar cases the ball passed through the left testicle, injuring the urethra, so that the patients passed urine for some time through the wounds in the urethra (as was stated in the case-book of Assistant-Surgeon Smith, 9th Lancers, who had medical charge of the men on the passage home); the fistulous opening in the canal closed entirely, and the natural passage remained undiminished in size, allowing of a full-sized catheter to pass with ease into the bladder. One of them was sent to duty, and the other to modified duty. The third case was from a spent round shot, which struck the man over the pubes without injuring the integuments, producing incontinence of urine. He still remains undisposed of.

Private Peter Forbes, aged 32. Wounded at Delhi, June 18, 1857, by a musket-ball which struck the left testicle, passed through the pubes and bladder, and made its exit posteriorly in the centre of the right hip. The left testicle was so much injured that it was removed the same day. He passed his urine for one month entirely through the wound.

April 10, 1858. A large bougie was passed with perfect ease.

20th. The sinus does not now appear to communicate with the urethra.

May 1st. Removed to-day a small piece of bone from the depth of the length of the forceps, in the pelvis. There is no communication between the sinus and the urinary passages.

10th. Another small piece of bone taken away from the same depth as the former piece.

13th. The wound remains in the same state; a piece of bone can be felt by the probe, very deep and apparently loose, but cannot be reached by the forceps.

June 4th. Succeeded in reaching and removing two pieces of bone, evidently from the internal surface of the ischium.

11th. There has been less discharge, and he is quite free from pain, and can walk about.

July 21, 1858. Wound quite healed. Modified duty.

75th Regt.—Private S. Young, wounded at Delhi, September 14, 1857, by a musket-ball which struck the left side of the penis, injuring the urethra and left testicle; then entered the inner side of the left thigh, and made its exit through the centre of the hip posteriorly. The left testicle came away shortly after, and he passed his urine through the wound in the side of the penis.

20th. All the wounds are now healed; No. 8 catheter can be passed with ease.

July 21, 1858. Duty.

88th Regt.—Private William Smith, wounded at Cawnpore, November 26, 1857, by a spent round shot, which caused a bruise over the symphysis of the pubes and outer side of the left thigh; has never since been able to retain his urine.

August 16, 1858. His urine passes constantly from him, without having the least control over it. He has been supplied with a patent urinal. He complains of weakness in his loins, but is otherwise in good health.

No. 2956. Cast of a section of a urinary calculus which had a musket-ball for a nucleus.—*Donor, Sir G. Ballingall, Edinburgh.*

The following case illustrates the tricks that soldiers play upon each other.

Private James Hussey, aged 25, 18th Regiment, had served abroad seven years, of which upwards of six were spent in China. At Hong Kong, on the 24th October, 1845, he was taken to the guard-room in a state of intoxication, and on becoming sensible he found a piece of cane, about a foot long, in the urethra, retained by a string tied round the penis, and the removal of which was attended with slight hemorrhage. About a month afterwards he complained of pain over the pubis and difficult micturition, the urine when passed being mixed with blood and mucus. On introducing a catheter into the bladder, a grating sensation was experienced.

He was admitted into Fort Pitt Hospital on the 19th May, 1847, in a very emaciated condition. His skin was dry and scaly; gums spongy and scorbutic, and he likewise suffered from diarrhœa, which attacked him at the time he was leaving China. He complained of constant and severe pain over the hypogastric region and along the course of the urethra; he was unable to retain his urine, which continually flowed from him in small quantities. On introducing a sound into the bladder, a large stone, supposed to be of soft consistence, was at once detected. His general health having considerably improved, and the diarrhœa having in a great measure been checked, the lateral operation of lithotomy was performed by Dr. Williamson, Staff-Surgeon. The patient had a favourable recovery. The man was not aware of a portion of cane having been driven into the bladder, nor was this circumstance known when the operation was commenced. No. 2004.—Portion of cane, being part of the stem of a tobacco-pipe removed from the bladder by the operation of lithotomy. It is $3\frac{3}{4}$ inches in length, and hollow in the centre, and was completely imbedded in the centre of a soft stone; the portions extracted must have weighed about two ounces; the fragments preserved weighed one ounce, and are composed of uric acid.

Class VIII.—Gunshot Wounds of the Upper Extremities.

Division 1.—*Simple Flesh Contusions and Wounds.*

Slight, 39; severe, 8. Total, 47.

Of these 30 have been sent to duty; 6 to modified duty; 6 invalided; and 5 remain undisposed of.

All were wounds by musket-ball, with the exception of 3 by round shot, 2 by shell, and 1 by slugs; 28 were wounded in the shoulder and arm, and 11 in the forearm and hand. The wounds were, with few exceptions, all healed, but in a number of cases there was more or less muscular contraction, and consequent loss of use and power in the arm, resulting from the patients' keeping the wounded limb in one particular position for months. In many cases the arm had become apparently perfectly useless, and in some cases even an incumbrance, so that I have been asked to remove it by amputation. This system of nursing their wounded limbs is brought about by trying at first to save themselves pain on any attempt at motion being made, and also from an idea that if they are invalided for a wound received in action they will be granted a higher pension than for any other disability.

In some the fingers were so contracted, and the nails so long, hard, and horny, resembling claws, that they had produced ulceration in the palm of the hand; to remedy this, the bath-man was supplied with a pair of strong scissors to keep the fingers of such patients in proper order.

In others the elbow-joint was contracted, distorted, and perfectly firm and rigid, and in a semi-bent position, and the fingers powerless from want of use.

The mode adopted for these contractions was simple, and consisted in forcible extension, the patient at the time being generally under the influence of chloroform; strong, straight, splints of different sizes were used; they were well padded, and covered with linen firmly sewed down. Before applying the splint, the arm was bandaged with a flannel roller, and the splints, as stated, were strong and of a good breadth, and also of such length as to extend beyond the bones included in the contraction. For instance, when the elbow-joint is contracted, the splint should extend from the fingers beyond the shoulder so as to afford plenty of leverage and purchase, as a very considerable degree of force has to be used. These splints were used almost daily on different patients, and with great success. The number of cases in which perfect cures were effected was great, and in others the condition of the limb was much improved. In none was there any serious injury or bad effect resulting from this process. Occasionally a considerable amount of inflammation and swelling follows, with vesication of the integuments; this always subsides under cold applications, and if the limb should again become contracted, the splint should be reapplied as soon as possible. In some cases a single application of the splint sufficed to straighten the contracted part, but more frequently the splint had to be applied several times, at intervals of a day or two. Sometimes the pain is so great that the patient cannot bear the application of the splint for more than a few hours. He ought, however, to be induced to keep it on as long as possible.

Of the 8 cases returned as severe, 3 were produced by round shot, causing severe laceration and destruction of the soft parts; 1 was by musket-ball through the biceps, along with 3 bayonet wounds of the shoulder, followed by sloughing; in 2 cases by a musket-ball through the arm, followed by sloughing; the last was a severe shell wound of the forearm.

DIVISION 2.—*With Contusion and partial Fracture of Long Bones, including Fracture of the Clavicle and Scapula.*

Under this head 30 have been admitted, of which 13 have been sent to duty; 4 to modified duty; 5 invalided; 1 died of pyemia; and 7 remain undisposed of.

All were produced by musket-ball, with the exception of 1 by a piece of a shell. 14 were injuries of the scapula; 4 of the clavicle; 6 of the humerus; 3 of the radius; and 3 of the ulna.

Of the 14 cases of partial fracture of the scapula, 6 have been sent to duty; 2 to modified duty; 2 invalided; and 4 remain undisposed of. The 4 remaining may be included amongst the invalided, which makes a total of 6 discharged the service.

In some cases the ball entered through the fold of the axilla, and passed directly through the scapula. In others the ball entered above the clavicle, and passed through the superior angle of the scapula. In one case the ball injured both scapulæ, passing from side to side; in another the ball seemed to have gone between the scapula and ribs. Fractures of the scapula are not dangerous unless they shatter the neck of the bone, or cause a fissure into the joint. Abscesses are apt to form under the fascia of the back, and require to be laid freely open by incision. Necrosis is not so frequent a result of gunshot fractures of the upper as of the lower extremity.

Of the 4 cases of partial fracture of the clavicle, 2 have been sent to duty; 1 invalided in consequence of loss of power in right arm; the fourth still remains undisposed of: in this case the aperture of entrance was healed on arrival here, but that of exit was still open, and led down to bare bone in the clavicle.

Of the 6 cases of partial fracture of the humerus, all occurred in the shaft of the bone; 1, as already stated, died of pyemia; 3 were sent to duty, and 2 invalided. The case of Private John Lloyd is interesting, as illustrating (Preparation No. 3629, see Plate VI., Fig. 1) the appearance of a partial fracture or indentation of a long bone, caused by a musket-ball, which was followed by necrosis of the part injured, while the remaining portion of the thickness of the shaft still continues intact; also the wound remaining open and suppurating, rendering the patient liable to blood-poisoning by the absorption of pus.

9th Lancers.—Private John Lloyd, wounded at Delhi, August 12, 1857, by a musket-ball in the right shoulder, which passed through on the inner side of the humerus, and made its exit on the posterior side of the arm. Both wounds healed before leaving India, but broke out on board ship.

August 2nd. The aperture of entrance is large, about an inch in diameter, and discharges freely. General health indifferent, and of a scorbutic tendency.

5th. He complained of dyspnœa; the wound looked sluggish; tongue coated; gums spongy; suffered from pains in the back and loins, especially in the right hypochondriac region.

7th. The dyspnœa had increased, and his cough was troublesome; the sputa were purulent, and very tenacious; on applying the stethoscope to the chest, mucous rales could be heard masking the heart's sounds; pain in the right side; pulse small and quick; epistaxis was so considerable as to weaken him greatly; slight diarrhœa.

9th. He still suffers from diarrhœa; very restless at night, seems to be in every respect worse.

10th. Complains greatly of pain in the right side; appetite very bad; suffers much from vomiting.

11th. Bowels not open to-day; his face looks anxious; eyes sunken; pulse very weak and quick; appetite entirely gone.

12th. Bowels not open for forty-eight hours; is getting

very low; complains greatly of pain in the left side; expectoration thick and purulent.

13th. Died.

Sectio Cadaveris, twenty hours after.—External Appearances.—The aperture of entrance of ball, about an inch in diameter, was observed to be situated on the front of the right shoulder, and on inserting a probe it was found to proceed backwards, between the upper part of the shaft of the humerus and the large vessels and nerves of the axilla, none of which were injured, and passed as far back as the integuments on the posterior fold of the axilla, where the aperture of exit was seen to be closed. The track of the ball was of a dark colour, and in a sloughing state, and contained three small pieces of necrosed bone. A portion of the shaft of the humerus, on its inner side, about two inches below its tuberosity, was bare, and denuded of periosteum, and carious. There is also a depression in this situation from loss of bony structure, where the ball had caused a partial fracture, No. 3629. *Cranium.*—Membranes of brain much congested; the brain otherwise healthy. *Thorax.*—There were five ounces of serum in the pericardium; heart healthy. The mucous membrane of the larynx, trachea, and bronchial tubes, as far as it could be traced into the lungs, of a deep purple colour, and highly congested; the right pleural cavity free from adhesions; the left pleural cavity slightly connected to the walls of the chest from recently effused lymph, a thin coating of which covered the inferior lobe. On making a section of the lungs, they were found œdematous; several small sacs, the size of a bean, containing deposits of pus, were found in the structure of the inferior lobe of the left lung, and the surrounding substance was somewhat condensed. *Abdomen.*—The liver was much enlarged, and of a dark colour, the structure being otherwise healthy; the gall-bladder was filled with a thin watery bile. The spleen was also greatly enlarged, the structure being soft and easily broken up. The kidneys were very much enlarged, and presented the appearance of granular degeneration in the second stage, some of the tubular portions having disappeared. The stomach and intestines were slightly congested, and of a dark slate colour from a carbonaceous deposit.

Of the 3 cases of partial fracture of the ulna, 2 have been sent to duty, and 1 to modified duty; 2 were in the shaft of the bone, 1 by a piece of shell, close to the elbow-joint, resulting in anchylosis.

61st Regt.—Edwin Carter, aged 37, wounded at Delhi,

September 15, 1857, by a piece of shell which struck the inner side of the right elbow-joint, a little below the olecranon, injuring the bone in the vicinity of the joint, without producing rupture of the skin; considerable pain and swelling of the joint ensued, which were relieved by incisions giving exit to a large quantity of pus. One large piece of bone came away. The wound did not heal for five months.

September 5th. Wound healed; forearm in a semi-bent position, and elbow-joint completely anchylosed.

October, 1858. Modified duty.

One case of partial fracture of the radius was sent to duty.

DIVISION 3.—*Simple Fracture of the Long Bones by Contusion from Round Shot.*

2 have been admitted, and 2 invalided; 1 was a case of simple fracture of the ulna, with contusion of the wrist, followed by abscesses in the hand; the other is a case of fracture of the clavicle, still ununited, with loss of pulsation and diminished temperature in the injured arm.

32nd Regt.—Private James Bailey, wounded at Lucknow, September 2, 1857, by a round shot, on the left side of the chest, breaking the first and second ribs, and centre of left clavicle, also contusing the shoulder.

July 13, 1858. The fracture of the clavicle is still ununited; has lost power in the arm, and cannot use the fingers; no pulse can be felt at the wrist, and the left arm is of a lower temperature than the right.

August 5, 1858. Invalided.

DIVISION 4.— *With Compound Fracture of the Humerus.*

17 have been admitted under this head. 3 have been sent to modified duty; 13 have been invalided; and 1 remains undisposed of. 1 was caused by a piece of a shell, and the others by musket-ball. All were fractured in the shaft of the bone, with two exceptions; 1 of them was through the head of the humerus, anchylosis of the shoulder-joint resulted; the other was through the surgical neck of the bone; 1 only remained unhealed on arrival here.

In almost every case of fracture implicating the humerus or bones of the forearm, there was great muscular contraction and rigidity of the tendons and ligaments around the elbow-joint, and the fingers were bent and contracted, requiring forcible extension to ameliorate their condition, and in some to effect a cure.

In compound fractures of the upper extremity primary amputation is never resorted to except in very severe and hopeless cases of gunshot wounds.

The following is a case of complete fracture of the humerus, with the ball lodged in the bone below the brachial artery. 53rd Regt.—Private Patrick Radding, aged 29, wounded, November 1, 1857, by a musket-ball, which entered on the outer side of the left humerus, about two inches above the elbow, and appears to have passed through the bone to the inner side, where it still remains imbedded in the bone; several pieces of bone have come away.

June 11, 1858. There is now a firm, hard substance on the inner side under the brachial artery, and he cannot straighten the arm in consequence of contraction of the biceps; there is a deep depression at the entrance of the ball. As the ball did not cause much annoyance, it was not considered advisable to cut down upon it, and remove it, particularly as the man was averse to the operation.

August 26th, 1858. Invalided.

The next is a case of fracture of the surgical neck of the humerus, the shoulder-joint remaining sound. 78th Regt.—Private Geo. Mathews, wounded at Lucknow, September 25, 1857, by a musket-ball, which entered in front of the left shoulder, through the anterior fold of the axilla, passed directly backwards, and came out at the posterior surface of the arm at the posterior margin of the deltoid behind the joint, causing a comminuted fracture at the surgical neck of the humerus; profuse suppuration ensued; several fragments of bone have come away.

July 11th. Apertures of entrance and exit of ball remain open; small pieces of bare bone can be felt; there is some enlargement of the bone at the seat of injury from deposition of new bone. The shoulder-joint is apparently sound, although he cannot move the arm, but he has perfect use of the forearm and hand.

The following is a case where the ball passed through the head of the humerus, followed by abscesses and anchylosis of the shoulder-joint. 75th Regt.—Corporal John Ryan, aged 31, wounded at Delhi, August 12, 1857, by a musket-ball, which entered the head of the left humerus, and passed out about two inches from the spinous process of the vertebra, between the seventh and eighth ribs; stated that he spat up blood for three weeks after; abscesses formed, and numerous pieces of bone came away from the shoulder.

July 20th, 1858. Wound healed; shoulder-joint anchylosed. It is not certain whether the lung was wounded or not.

October 6, 1858. Invalided.

The following is a case of ununited fracture of the humerus, from India, in an officer. Major M. had his right humerus severely shattered in its middle third by a musket-ball, in June, 1858, at Juydespore; the shot was fired by a Sepoy who was within a few yards of him. Several pieces of bone came away at the time, and since then a considerable number of small pieces.

March, 1859. There is now a space of about two inches between the ends of the bones, no union having taken place, and there is a slight discharge from a sinus which remains open. There still appear to be some necrosed portions of bone to come away; and it is not thought advisable at the present time to perform any operation with the view of effecting union.

No. 2924. Shows deficiency of a large portion of the lower part of the shaft of the humerus, from necrosis, in consequence of gunshot wound.

No. 2925. Humerus, the shaft of which has been shattered by gunshot, and firmly consolidated by osseous matter; a large splinter, which was completely detached, has become perfectly united to the shaft. From Patrick Waldron, 87th Regt., who received a fracture of the arm in the Burmese war. The ball entered between the outer edge of the biceps and insertion of the deltoid, passed through the os humeri and triceps, and made its exit on the inner side of the arm. The power of the limb was never restored; he subsequently died of apoplexy. When the arm was examined after death the radial nerve was found to have been wounded, and at the injured part was converted into a cartilaginous substance.

b.—With Compound Fracture of the Radius.

18 have been admitted. 1 has been sent to duty; 2 to modified duty; 14 invalided. 1 was produced by a piece of a shell, close to the elbow-joint, followed by anchylosis; and the others by musket-ball; only 1 remained unhealed.

In some of these cases there was great comminution of bone and loss of substance. In some instances as much as two and three inches of the shaft were deficient, and in all there was more or less contraction of the fingers, and consequent impaired use of the hand and forearm, so as to render the men unfit for service. In 2 cases the fracture was close to the wrist-joint; in 1 case the fracture remained ununited, although the ends of the bone were in contact; in one the ball was supposed to be lodged and impacted in the bone, and was cut down upon, but could not be found.

The following is a case of fracture of the radius, with probable injury of the median nerve.

88th Regt.—Private Robert Buchanan, aged 20, wounded November 26, 1857, by a musket-ball, which entered on the anterior suface of the forearm, about three inches below the elbow-joint, and passed out on the posterior surface, opposite to the place of entrance; the radius was fractured, and several pieces of bone have come away; the median nerve has also, probably, been wounded.

July 11, 1858. He has now completely lost the power of motion and sensation in the hand, which hangs powerless by the side, and the lower extremity of the ulna projects as if the hand was partly dislocated.

July 31, 1858. Invalided.

The next case is one of severe comminution, with loss of about two and a half inches of the shaft of the bone.

60th Rifles (1st Battalion).—Private John Kerr, aged 19, wounded at Delhi, June 14, 1857, by a musket-ball, causing a compound comminuted fracture of the right radius about its middle, doing also much injury to the flexor tendons; several pieces of bone were taken away at the time.

July 20, 1858. Wound healed; there is loss of a portion of the shaft of the radius for about two and a half inches; he cannot use the fingers, or pronate or supinate the hand.

July 21, 1858. Invalided.

No. 2926. Radius, the shaft of which has been fractured by a gunshot, and reunited by new osseous matter, and firmly consolidated thereby to the ulna.

c.—With Compound Fracture of the Ulna.

7 have been admitted, of whom 2 have been sent to duty; 1 to modified duty; and 3 invalided; and 1 remains. All were by musket-ball, and were healed on arrival. In 1 case ligature of the radial artery had been performed on account of sloughing.

d.—With Compound Fracture of the Radius and Ulna.

3 have been admitted. 1 sent to duty, and 2 invalided. In 1 of these cases the fracture of both bones was produced by a piece of telegraph rod, which the mutineers fired when they became short of ammunition. The fracture was in the lower third near the wrist. In the other case the fracture was caused by the soldier falling from his horse in action.

DIVISION 5.—*Penetrating, perforating, or lacerating the several Structures of the Carpus and Metacarpus.*

Under this head there have been 26 admissions, of which 5 have been sent to duty; 7 to modified duty; and 13 invalided; 1 remains undisposed of. The proportion invalided in these injuries is great, and shows their severity. In some cases the ball completely perforated the carpus or metacarpus; in others it struck the bone in a slanting direction, and passed out, producing more or less injury to the bones, tendons, and ligaments, so that in almost every case there was contraction and rigidity of parts, with distortion, want of power, and otherwise impaired use of the hand and fingers resulting. Whenever it was requisite, forcible extension was resorted to. In two cases the wrist-joint was anchylosed. In one case the ball still remains in the fleshy part between the thumb and fore-finger, and it was not thought expedient to cut down upon it and remove it, in consequence of its not producing much inconvenience, and also from the patient objecting to the operation, fearing that he might be attacked with lock-jaw, and especially as he was otherwise strong and healthy.

84th Regt.—Private Thomas Rushworth, aged 28, wounded at Lucknow, November 17, 1857, by a musket-ball, in the left wrist, which entered on the front nearly in the centre, passed directly through, and made its exit on the posterior side; several pieces of the carpal bones were removed at the time, and great swelling of the hand ensued.

August 16, 1858. Wounds healed; there is anchylosis of the wrist-joint, with impaired use of the hand.

September 2, 1858. Sent to modified duty.

DIVISION 6.—*Dividing or lacerating the several Structures of the Carpus and Metacarpus.*

9 have been admitted; 4 have been sent to duty; 2 invalided; and 3 remain.

CLASS IX.—GUNSHOT WOUNDS OF THE LOWER EXTREMITIES.

DIVISION 1.—*Simple Flesh Contusions and Wounds.*

Slight, 87; severe, 13; total, 100.

Of the total 100 cases, 63 have been sent to duty; 6 to modified duty; 13 invalided; and 18 remain undisposed of.

On comparing the number of gunshot wounds of the upper with that of the lower extremities, it will be noticed that they are very nearly the same, viz., 159 in the upper, and 162 in the lower. There is, however, a considerable difference as to the number of flesh gunshot wounds, there being 100 in the lower, and only 47 in the upper extremities. 5 were shell wounds; 8 by grape-shot; 1 by a brick-bat; 1 by a rifle-ball; and the remainder by musket-ball. 12 were wounded in the hip; 26 in the thigh: and 62 in the leg. In 2 cases balls were extricated from the fleshy part of the thigh, at Fort Pitt; and in another case from the perineum, immediately over the bulb of the urethra, the ball having entered on the outer side of the thigh, opposite the trochanter major; in 3 cases the wounds were very close to the femoral artery; and in 1 the ball still remains in the thigh. This man is returned under "Amputation of the Finger," but the other wound is interesting, and is noticed in this place: the ball must have grazed the femoral artery and vein; on inserting a probe into the fistulous opening, the ball could be distinctly felt deep behind the artery. Of the 13 severe cases, 1 was by a ball which is lodged in the tuberosity of the ischium; 2 were from round shot in the thigh, followed by sloughing: several were ball and shell wounds in the thigh, followed by sloughing; 1 was by a rifle-ball in the thigh; 1 by a ball in the thigh close to the femoral artery, injuring the sciatic nerve; and in 5 cases the wounds were from balls in the fleshy parts of the leg, followed by sloughing.

In a number of cases there was great contraction and rigidity of the hamstring muscles and ligaments around the knee-joint, also in the muscles of the calf, and around the ankle-joint, requiring forcible extension. Many of them, on arrival, walked with crutches, the leg suspended in slings, and the foot pushed out behind; the crutches were taken from them, and the limbs placed in splints and extended; and with the same results as in the upper extremity, the greater number being much improved in condition, and several perfectly cured.

The very indolent character of open sores after gunshot wounds is worthy of remark. The men were apparently in good health, had lived well both in India and on board ship, and were generally untainted with scurvy; still, the ulcers resisted every mode of treatment,—lotions of every description, blisters, strapping, incisions, filling them with wax, &c.,—nothing would induce granulations, or a healthy action.

The following is a case where a ball entered posteriorly in the centre of the buttocks, and lodged in or near the pubes; the ball could not be felt by the finger from the perineum, but it was detected by the long probe through the aperture in the hip. 10th Regt.—Private John Ferguson, wounded at Benares, June 4, 1857, by a musket-ball, which entered the centre of the right buttock, and passed forwards and downwards, and is now lodged in or near the ramus of the pubes.

July 13th. The aperture of entrance on the centre of the right hip is still open, and the ordinary probe goes in its entire length without feeling any foreign body; the long probe can detect the ball lying near the pubes.

July 17, 1858. Invalided.

In the following case the ball must have grazed, or at least passed very close to the femoral artery, and lodged deep beneath it. 84th Regt.—Private Thomas Bulger, aged 33, wounded at Cawnpore, November 16, 1857, by a musket-ball, which struck him on the left hand, fracturing the first, second, and third fingers, and then passed through the anterior and outer part of the upper third of the left thigh from behind forwards. Wounded by a second musket-ball in the anterior aspect of the left thigh, the ball entering about three inches below Poupart's ligament, close to the course of the femoral artery, where it lodged. Amputation of the fore and middle fingers, between the first and second phalanges, was performed four days after.

August 16th. Covering of stumps of fingers good; motions of ring and little fingers impaired. The wound where the ball entered still remains open; there is only a small sinus, through which the ball can be felt, situated close to the inner side of the femoral vein; attempts were made to dilate the wound by tents, as it would have been rather hazardous to cut down upon it, being so very near the femoral artery and vein; the man objected strongly to have an incision made for its removal, and, as the wound had closed, he was discharged the service, October 15, 1858, on account of loss of fingers by amputation, under which head he is included in the Return, although noticed in this place for the wound in the thigh.

DIVISION 2.—*With Contusion and partial Fracture of Long-Bones, and of the Bones of the Pelvis, in their relation to the Lower Extremities.*

28 have been admitted, of whom 8 have been sent to duty, 4 to modified duty, 10 invalided, and 6 remain undisposed of. 5 were partial fractures of the ilium, 3 in the thigh, 14 in the tibia, and 5 in the fibula; 13 were caused by ball, 3 by grape, 1 by round-shot, and 1 by shell. Of the 5 cases of fracture of the ilium, several were very severe; in 2 the balls were supposed still to remain impacted in the ilium, but causing no inconvenience; in 1 a portion of bone, 2 inches in diameter, came away by necrosis; of the 3 cases of wounds in the thigh, in 2 of them there was only slight injury to the femur; in the third case the ball entered in the popliteal space, and anchylosis of the knee-joint resulted; of the 14 wounded in the leg, there was 1 where the ball fractured the tibia, with, probably, a split into the ankle-joint; in 1 case sloughing followed, requiring ligature of the posterior tibial artery; in 1 a round-shot tore the soft parts extensively; and in 1 the greater portion of the tibia became necrosed, and was taken away. In a number of cases there was considerable contraction of the knee and leg.

The following is a case where a ball is said to be firmly impacted in the ilium. 10th Regt.—Private Robert Sherlock, wounded at Benares, June 4, 1857, by a musket-ball, which entered about two inches below the crest of the ilium, and is firmly impacted in the bone, as stated in the document. At a consultation held on November 17, 1857, at Dinapore, it was decided that at present an operation was not advisable.

July 12, 1858. Wound healed; ball cannot be felt through the soft parts, and it causes no uneasiness or pain to the man.

July 13, 1858. Sent to duty.

The next is a case of fracture of the ilium by grape-shot, followed by necrosis.

Preparation No. 3627 is the portion of the external table of the ilium, about two inches in diameter, which was removed from the following subject. 88th Regt.—Private Martin Ford, aged 20, wounded at Cawnpore, November 26, 1857, by a grape-shot, on the crest of the right ilium, immediately above the anterior and superior spinous process, where it lodged, and was extracted two days after; several pieces of necrosed bones have come away.

October 10, 1858. Wounds healed; there is a deep adherent cicatrix over the outer side of the hip, with stiffness and contraction of muscles.

October 15, 1858. Modified duty.

The following case is an example of a wound near a joint, producing such severe inflammation of the ligamentous structure and of the joint itself, as to cause anchylosis. This case was placed under this Division, as it was thought probable there was more or less injury to the bone, although it was stated in the report of the case that there was not any fracture.

60th Rifles (1st Battalion).—Private Edmund Miller, wounded at Delhi, September 14, 1857, by a musket-ball, which struck the centre of the popliteal space, but, as far as could be observed at the time, not entering the joint or causing any fracture; great swelling and effusion occurred, with considerable disturbance, and excessive pain on moving the limb, or even the mildest manipulation. The ball was extracted, with some difficulty, from the aperture of entrance, which rapidly healed, and again broke out.

July 20, 1858. Left knee anchylosed, but he is still able to walk.

July 22, 1858. Invalided.

The following case shows extensive necrosis of the tibia, which is a frequent result of injury or partial fracture of this bone. 75th Regt.—Private George Steptoe, wounded at Delhi, September 14, 1857, by a musket-ball in the left leg, which entered immediately below the tubercle of the tibia, and passed out on the outer side of the leg at its upper third; several pieces of bone came away from both wounds.

July 20, 1858. Exit wound healed, entrance aperture still open, and several other sinuses leading down to necrosed bone; tibia enlarged; integument livid and discoloured.

26th. Two pieces of bone, about two inches in length, were extracted from the centre of the tibia, at Fort Pitt.

Undisposed of.

The last case in this Division is an example of a longitudinal fracture into the ankle-joint, followed by anchylosis.

5th Regt.—Private William Burrowes, wounded at Juydespore, August 12, 1857, by a spent musket-ball, on the inner side of the right leg, about one inch above the ankle-joint; it was extracted immediately after by pulling out the sock and trowsers, which had been carried in with it; the tibia seems to have been splintered longitudinally into the ankle-joint.

September 26, 1858. Wound healed; ankle-joint anchylosed; there is a slight depression along the front of the lower third of the tibia; he walks lame.

November 21, 1858. Invalided.

Division 3.—*With Simple Fracture of Long Bones by contusion of Round Shot.*

One was admitted, and is returned under "Amputations of the Leg." (M'Crea, page 101.)

Division 4.—*With Compound Fracture of Femur.*

8 have been admitted from India, of whom 2 have been sent to modified duty, 5 invalided, and 1 died. 1 double fracture, —one fracture being at the upper third, and one at the middle third; fracture at the upper third in 4; at the middle third in 3. By musket-ball in 7; by round-shot in 1; musket-ball lodged in 3; wound healed on arrival in 5; Limb three inches shorter in 3, two and a half inches shorter in 1, one and a half inches shorter in 2, and one inch shorter in 2 instances.

Besides these 8 cases there is 1 (Private M'Crea[a]) of a *simple* fracture of the lower third of the femur, by round-shot, received in action, where amputation of the leg was performed at the tubercle of the tibia.

It is taught by most military surgeons that, as a rule, immediate amputation should be performed in all compound comminuted fractures of the femur; and that by attempting to save limbs more patients have lost their lives. It is also recommended in all cases of gunshot fractures of the middle and lower thirds of the femur, but especially in the middle third, that amputation should be performed; but in the same injury in the upper third, the limb should be preserved, as it has been found that amputation in the upper third of the thigh is almost certainly fatal, so that such a severe operation is not considered advisable when the prospect of success is so small, and by retaining the limb the patient is much more comfortable, with equal chances of saving his life. It may be mentioned that one case of amputation of the upper third of the thigh arrived from India: it was so high up that the stump could not be retained in the bucket of the artificial limb.

It appears from the result of the Schleswig Holstein war, that a considerable number of these cases were preserved with very useful limbs. The number which have arrived from India

[a] The history of this case will be found under "Amputation of the Leg."

is very large in proportion, viz., 8 cases of compound comminuted fracture of the femur to the total wounded, 603. Of 2296 discharged the service at Chatham, in consequence of wounds received in the Crimean war, there were only 8 recoveries with the limb on. The success of these cases from India may, in part, be attributed by some surgeons to the ball of the old musket being smaller, and not producing such a severe fracture as that used by the Russians during the late war, but more to the dooley as a means of conveyance, and in part to the army having been better supplied with good food, clothing, &c.

Generally cases of gunshot wounds progress more favourably in hot than in very cold climates, especially when great attention is paid to cleanliness. These fractures are, however, in my opinion, as severe as could be caused by any Russian ball, viz., in M'Carter's case, produced by round-shot, and Carty's, where there was a double fracture.[a] And, looking at these cases, it appears to be still an open question as to the necessity of immediate amputation in all cases of gun-shot fractures of the femur. When the fracture is close to the knee, or if the bone is split into the joint, amputation will be necessary; when the bone is simply fractured, and not splintered to any great extent, the ball having traversed the limb, it seems to be advisable, under favourable circumstances as to after-treatment, to try and save the limb at whatever part of the bone the fracture has taken place; when the femur is more extensively shattered, recourse must, of necessity, be had to amputation. A great deal must also depend upon the kind of projectile: when from round-shot, there is generally great comminution, and little hope can be entertained of saving the limb; but recoveries under such unfavourable circumstances do occasionally take place, as illustrated by the case of M'Carter, 64th Regiment. The fact that three men were sent to modified duty shows that they must have retained very useful limbs, so as to be able to carry messages and to act as orderlies: more than three might have been sent, as far as the condition of the leg was concerned.

The case of Carty, 64th Regiment, is interesting as showing a double fracture, both firmly united, and the ball supposed to be lodged.

Ashworth had recovered with such a strong useful leg, that, if it had not been for the shortening of the limb, he might have gone to his duty in the ranks.

[a] Compare these cases with preparation No. 2939, Plate VII., Fig. 1, p. 73, where the fracture was produced by *two* minie bullets.

Hewitt had also a very useful limb, and would have been sent to modified duty if he had not been close upon ten years' service, when he could have claimed his discharge.

Collins also retained a very useful limb, and could walk a long distance with a stick; he was discharged by Horse Guards' order, after having been sent to modified duty.

Burke has also a very good limb, and is at modified duty.

Walmsley (death) is very interesting, as showing strong bony union at the trochanter, with the ball lodged between the fractured ends.

Hunter is able to walk about with very little lameness, and the sinus discharges very little. There appears to be a very extensive deposition of new bone, with thickening of the lower third of the femur, and central necrosis; the new bone extends so low as to encroach somewhat on the motions of the knee.

They were all, as far as can be ascertained, treated by the long splint, with the exception of M'Carter and Burke, who used M'Intyre's splint for some time.

The advantage of the dooley over the best constructed ambulance, for the conveyance of sick and wounded over rough roads during active military operations, is well shown in the result of these cases of compound comminuted fracture of the femur. All regiments in India have a certain proportion of dooleys and dooley-bearers attached to them permanently in the time of peace, and when on the line of march and on active service they are, of course, increased. Why should not Government enlist and organize in India a corps of trained dooley-bearers for service with our regiments in European wars.

This appears to me to be a measure which could be carried out without much difficulty, if sufficient inducements as to pay, good treatment when in the service, and the promise of a pension when discharged, and sent back to their homes in India, were held out to them.

In the following case there was extensive laceration of the soft parts, and severe comminution of bone; large portions of necrosed bones were removed. The wound had never entirely healed; the limb was two inches and a quarter shorter than the other.

64th Regt.—Private William M'Carter, aged 26, nine years' service, was wounded on February 8, 1857, at Kooshat, in Persia, by a spent ball, which struck the outer and anterior aspect of the middle third of the right thigh, producing a severe comminuted fracture of the femur, with extensive laceration of the soft parts. The thigh was protected temporarily by a single straight splint on the outside. On the following morning the limb was put on a M'Intyre's splint, with two side splints in addition; considerable inflammation followed, with great swelling and profuse discharge, and constitutional disturbance. He remained in bed until May 6th, when he embarked for Bombay, when the wound was still discharging a good deal.

Four large and several smaller pieces of bone have come away at different times; abscesses have frequently formed on the posterior aspect of the thigh; and on one occasion a large piece of bone was removed from it.

Fort Pitt, May 4, 1858. General health good; fracture firmly united, but the bone is curved outwards; the original wound has never entirely closed, and there are now two sinuses leading down to bare bone.

18th. The necrosed portion of bone, about one inch in length, was removed; the limb was two and a quarter inches shorter than its fellow; on standing up, the great toe and next one touched the ground, and the heel is raised three and a quarter inches.

29th. Wounds nearly healed; can bear his weight upon the limb, and walk about, with the aid of a stick, without crutches. On the whole, he has a very useful limb, much preferable to any artificial one.

30th. Invalided.

In the next case there was a double fracture, both firmly united, the ball still remaining in; the limb is two and a half inches shortened; still, he walks so well that he has been sent to modified duty.

64th Regt.—Private Patrick Carty, aged 28, wounded at Lucknow by a musket-ball, which struck him, while in the erect position, on the right thigh, on its posterior surface, about five inches below the superior spinous process of the ilium; the ball, it is stated, still remains in the thigh. After being wounded, he remained at the village of Amoo for three days, with his thigh bound up tightly (he states) with short splints placed round the limb; on the fourth day he was removed to hospital at Cawnpore. Eighteen days after the wound was inflicted, he had a long splint put on, and was placed on a hard mattress; he remained in hospital at Cawnpore twenty-four days, and was then carried to Allahabad, the journey occupying eight days; he remained in hospital at Allahabad for one month, and was then conveyed to Calcutta in a steam-vessel; he remained in hospital at Calcutta for two months and eight days; the splint was removed after he had been in hospital at Calcutta one month; and on his embarking for England, on January 8, 1858, he was able to move about tolerably well with the aid of crutches; he states that during the voyage home he gained strength in the limb very rapidly.

June 25, 1858. The femur appears to have been fractured in two places: the upper fracture is just below the spot where the ball entered, a projection of a fractured end of the bone is distinctly felt there, and another projection of a fractured end of bone is felt at the outer and middle part of the thigh; there is also a small tumour on the outer side of the thigh, below the strong fascia, which is only movable when the muscles are relaxed: this may, probably, be the ball; the limb is shortened to the extent of two and a half inches; he can now walk for a short distance with very little lameness, without crutches or stick, and states that he does not suffer any pain unless he gets on uneven ground; his general health is good.

September 6, 1858. Sent to modified duty.

December 22nd. Invalided.

In the two following cases the fracture was in the upper third; the broken limbs were one and a half inches shortened, and they had become nearly as strong as the other legs.

53rd Regt.—Private John Ashworth, aged 29, wounded November 1, 1857, by a musket-ball, which entered two inches below the great trochanter, and emerged in the front of the thigh at its upper third, having in its course fractured the bone; the limb is one and a half inches shorter than the other.

July 14, 1858. Wounds healed; complains of weakness in the limb, but is able to walk about without the assistance of a stick.

September 6th. Sent to modified duty.

52nd Regt.—Private Joseph Hewitt, aged 27, wounded July 12th, at Goodispore, by a musket-ball, which entered on the anterior aspect of the upper third of the left thigh, and fractured the femur, the ball was cut out in the lower part of the gluteus muscles six weeks after.

July 20, 1858. Wound healed; the fractured ends of the bones overlap; the leg is now an inch and a half shorter than the other, and he cannot put his heel to the ground. It is a good cure, and he still retains a very useful limb; no pieces of bone came away; long splint used.

22nd. Invalided.

The following is a case of fracture of the upper third; the ends of the bones overlap considerably; the limb is shortened two and a half inches, and the ball lodged.

75th Regt.—Private Edward Collins, wounded at Delhi,

June 8, 1857, by a musket-ball, which entered the upper and outer side of the right thigh, and lodged, fracturing the femur; ball extracted; a piece of bone came away.

July 20th. Wound healed; right leg about two and a half inches shorter than left; femur bent; fractured ends of bone overlap, and there is abundant deposition of new bone; the long splint was used. Has a good useful limb, and can walk a long distance.

September 6, 1858. Sent to modified duty.

October 6th, 1858. Invalided by an order from the Horse Guards.

In the next case the fracture is between the middle and lower thirds of the femur; limb shortened one and a half inches.

53rd Regt.—Private James Burke, wounded at Lucknow, November 16, 1857, by a musket-ball, which entered the front of the left thigh, about the junction of the lower with the middle third, fracturing the femur, and passing inwards and backwards; it was cut out two days after in the inner side of the thigh; no piece of bone came away. Was sent back to Cawnpore in a dooley, and his leg retained in the long splint; went from Cawnpore, in a hackney, to Allahabad, on the 2nd December, and arrived there on the 10th, and shortly after the limb was put on a double-inclined plane, and finally upon the long splint; was unable to bear his weight on the limb until April, 1858.

August 16, 1858. Wounds healed; the fracture is united, but the ends overlap on the outer side, and the left leg is about one and a half inches shorter than the right; he can bend the knee-joint, and has a very useful limb, being able to walk tolerably well.

September 6, 1858. Sent to modified duty.

The following fatal case shows that it is often impossible to find out by what description of missile the wound is produced, as the document stated that the fracture was caused by a portion of shell, and a ball is seen to be lodged between the united ends of the bones. It also appears that there were two apertures, one of entrance and one of exit; so that he must have been wounded by two projectiles,—one, the ball, lodged; and the other, probably a portion of shell, perforated the limb. The preparation also shows the state of the parts twelve months after the injury. In such a case as this, excision at the hip might have been advisable.

60th Rifles (1st Battalion).—Sergeant Hugh Walmsley, aged 30, was taken into hospital at Gravesend from on board ship, being unable to proceed to Fort Pitt with the remainder of the invalids from India. Was wounded July 4, 1857, at Delhi, by a musket-ball, the ball entering about the upper third of the left thigh upon the outer side, and making its way out or through on the inner side, shattering the bone, some fragments of which have come away since he had been on board ship; on his arrival the wound was still open and discharging profusely; dead bone was easily detected by introducing the probe; was emaciated in the extreme, and suffering from chronic diarrhœa of a very obstinate character; the diarrhœa continued after his landing, and was eventually the cause of his death.

Post-mortem.—Body.—The marks of entrance and exit of a musket-ball on the inner and outer side of the upper third of right thigh; the limb was much shortened and distorted to the extent of about three inches, the great toe resting upon the instep of the opposite side. *Thorax.*—Heart and lungs both healthy. *Abdomen.*—Liver healthy, with the exception of one or two whitened patches on its surface; the lower portion of the large intestines was congested, and the mucous membrane showed marks of old ulceration, the result of chronic dysentery. Preparation No. 3624 (see Plate VI., Fig. 2). Right femur, showing a comminuted fracture of the upper third, immediately below the trochanter; the fracture extends from the great trochanter obliquely, downwards and inwards, for an inch below the smaller trochanter; the extremity of the lower end of the fractured bone is on a level with the great trochanter; the extremities of the fractured ends of the bones are very firmly united by extensive depositions of new bone, and there is a large cavity between the ends, in which there is a round musket-ball, and a large aperture leading to it on the outer side, where it entered; on this side there is also a large irregular lamina of necrosed bone.

The last is a case of fracture between the middle and lower thirds, followed by necrosis, and extensive deposition of new bone so as in some measure to impede the motion of the knee-joint.

93rd Regt.—Private Samuel Hunter, aged 24, wounded at Lucknow, November 1, 1857, by a musket-ball, which struck the outer side of the left thigh, at the juncture of the middle and lower third, fracturing the femur, and passed out on the inner side; a number of pieces of necrosed bone have come away. Was sent in a dooley to Futtehpore, where he remained nine days; the limb being placed in a short splint along both sides; was then sent by dooley to Allahabad, where the long splint was applied, and retained four months.

September 26, 1858. Aperture of entrance and exit healed;

Pl. VI

Fig. 1.

3629

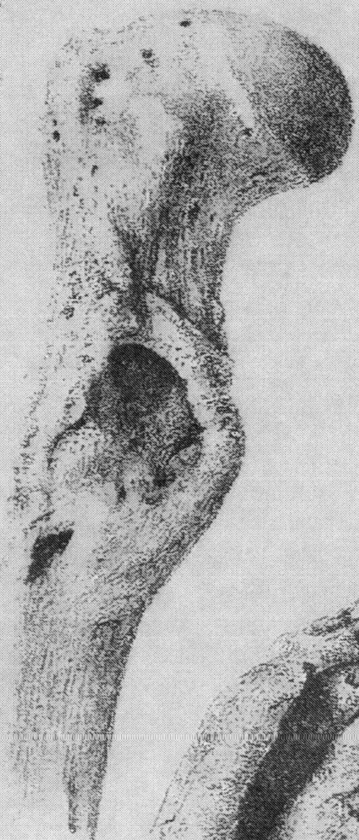

Fig. 2.

3624

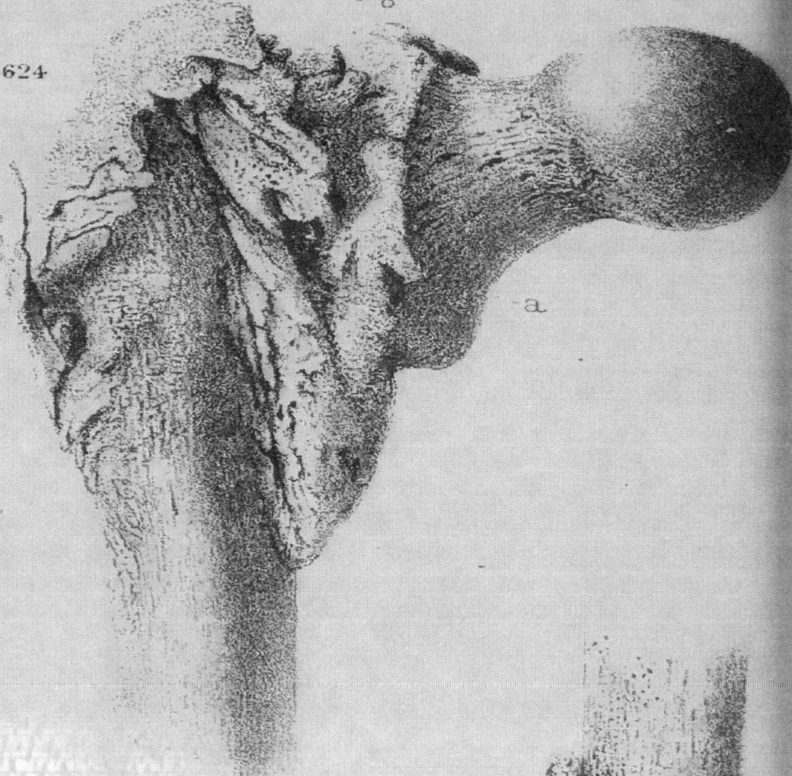

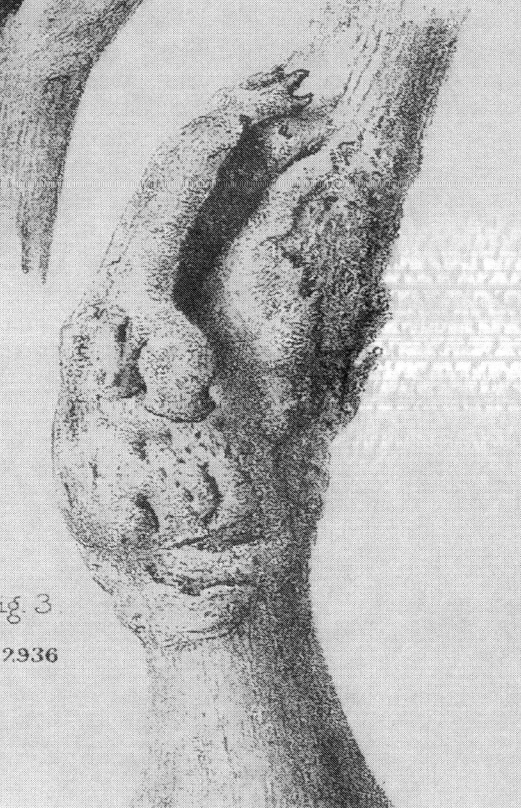

Fig. 3.

2936

Fig. 4

2937

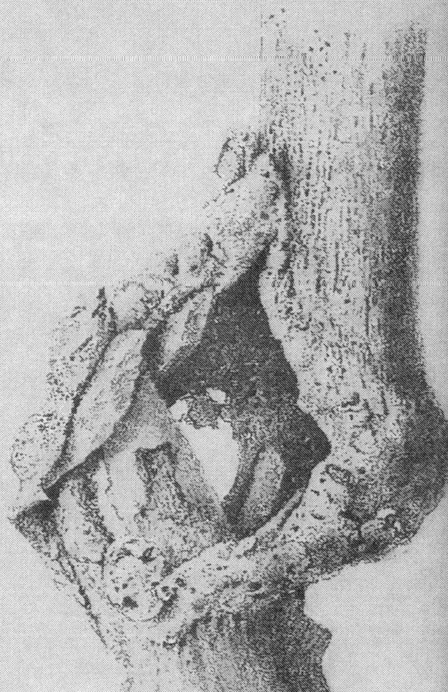

Fig. 2. a. Ball lodged. b. Portion of necrosed bone.

G. H. Ford. W. West imp.

there is a sinus on the outer and posterior aspect of the middle and lower third of the thigh, through one of which bone can be detected; the left leg is one inch shorter than the other, and there is great deposition of callus around the fractured ends of the bone, which have been considerably displaced.

September 5, 1858. Invalided.

The three following preparations, Nos. 2936, 2937, 2938, where the patient survived for many months, show the great amount of comminution which takes place, even from the old ball, and the amount of distortion which unavoidably ensues from the impossibility of keeping up the requisite degree of extension, with the consequent necrosis of portions of bone, and the large quantity of callus which is thrown out. No. 2936 shows that the inflammation must have extended to the knee-joint, the patella having become anchylosed to the femur, with absorption of the cartilages. In No. 2937 there are several large portions of bone, dead, and in process of separation. No. 2938 shows an immense large comminuted portion lying behind, with very great displacement and shortening, with very profuse depositions of new osseous matter.

The preparations Nos. 2936 and 2938 were from patients who were wounded at Ferozeshah.

No. 2936 (see Plate VI., Fig. 3). Comminuted fracture at the middle and lower third of the left femur, from gunshot. The bone is much distorted, and the lower portion is turned inwards; there is a large fragment lying in the posterior aspect, and the fractured extremities are united by a very abundant deposition of new osseous matter, in the centre of which are two portions of necrosed bone, firmly attached to the new bony matter. The patella is anchylosed to the femur, and the cartilage on the latter is absorbed. The patient died twelve months after the accident, from pneumonia. Taken from Private James Hewitt, 29th Regiment, aged 25; seven years' service, of which four years in India; received a gunshot wound at Ferozepore, December 21, 1845; the ball passed through the left thigh, fracturing the femur, and lodged in the right, from which it was extracted. Admitted into Fort Pitt General Hospital, September 28, 1846. There were two depressions on the left thigh. On October 7th erysipelas attacked this thigh; on the 11th, incisions were made on its inner side, from which a piece of exfoliated bone was extracted. From this date to the beginning of November the erysipelas had gradually extended to the foot, and had given rise to great constitutional disturbance. Openings were at different times made to give exit to large quantities of pus. There was shortening of the limb to the extent of four and a half inches, and four openings in the thigh, one on the outer side, through which the probe reached the bone in a denuded state.

December 27th. He was attacked with acute pain in the left side, at the lower border of the true ribs, accompanied by cough and difficulty of breathing. Expectoration not coloured; on the left side there was dulness, and coarse crepitation heard.

He gradually became weaker, and died January 2, 1847.

Sectio Cadaveris.—External Appearances.—Body much emaciated; left leg much swollen, and four and a half inches shorter than the other; on making an incision into the affected limb, the sub-cutaneous fat and areolar tissue were thickened, and infiltrated with serum; on laying open the outer sinus there issued a large quantity of dark-coloured pus; underneath this opening, and lying close upon the bone, was found the flattened remains of a musket-ball. The left pleural cavity contained two ounces of turbid serum, in which were floating flakes and masses of lymph; the pulmonary and costal pleura was highly vascular, and coated with a recent layer of lymph, which was easily detached. The lower lobe was condensed, and sank in water; a section presented the usual appearance of grey hepatization, softened and broke down, and infiltrated with pus. Right lung healthy.

No. 2937 (see Plate VI., Fig. 4). Gunshot fracture of the left thigh. The ends of the bones are very much displaced, but united by new bony deposit, which forms a large cavity; the end of the lower portion of the femur is necrosed and in progress of being separated; there are also several other portions of necrosed bone, either partially separated or bound down by the new bone; a comminuted portion of bone is situated on the outside, attached to the others by bony union.

No. 2938 (see Plate VII., Fig. 3). Lower part of the right femur, showing an extensive comminuted fracture from gunshot. The broken ends are much displaced; the lower portion lies to the inner side of the upper, having been drawn upwards and inwards by the action of the muscles; the limb must have been shortened to the extent of three or four inches; there is a large fragment at the posterior part of the preparation, which is united to the two fractured ends, but particularly to the lower portion, by a very abundant deposition of new osseous matter; there is a large cavity between the posterior fragment and the lower portion of the femur; the upper extremity of the fracture lies to the outer side of the lower, the extreme end of which is sharp and pointed, having been fractured obliquely, and, probably, protruded through the skin. From an officer

Pl. VII.

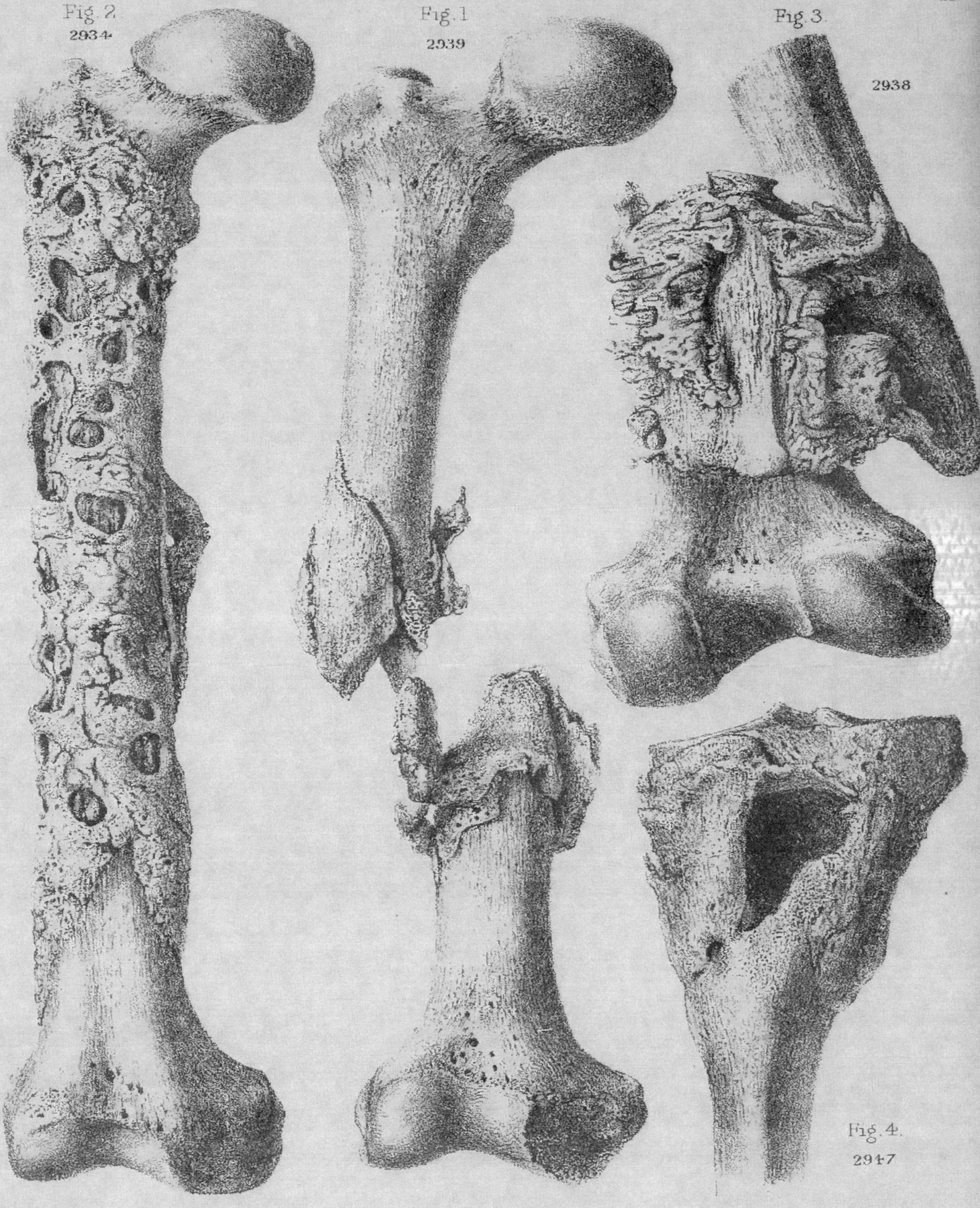

C. H. Ford. W West imp.

who received compound fracture of the thigh from gunshot, at Ferozeshah, and afterwards died of phthisis pulmonalis.

The preparation No. 2939 is a good specimen of ununited fracture at the middle of the femur, and shows the amount of comminution which follows from *two* conical balls, and also the deteriorated state of the patient's constitution, very little callus having been thrown out. The bone in this case is not nearly so extensively comminuted as in preparations Nos. 2936, 2937, and 2938, which were produced by the old round ball. This specimen is also an excellent example, showing the care which is requisite in examining gunshot wounds, either before inflammation has set in, or when operative measures have become necessary. In this case *two* minie balls had entered the limb; one of them was loosened by the suppurative process, and was extracted, and the other was found, on post-mortem examination, lying between the ends of the ununited fracture. The ball is also seen to be enclosed between the ends of the united fractures in the case of Walmesley, page 69. The same has been noticed in the Report on the Wounded from the Crimea, p. 362. No. 2939 (see Plate VII., Fig. 1). Gun-shot fracture in the centre of the right femur; bone much comminuted, and the extremities ununited and overlapping. The comminuted pieces are united by new bony deposit, and there are also several portions necrosed. Taken from Peter M'Donald, 42nd Highlanders, who was wounded on the Alma by a musket-shot, and sent to Scutari, when he was much reduced in strength, and the limb very much swelled, and discharging freely. After some time a musket-ball was discovered and removed; the swelling reduced, the sinuses closed, and he was enabled to move about with crutches. About a week after, the limb again swelled, irritative fever ensued, and the man died. On examining the limb, another minie-ball was found in the cavity between the ends of the bones, chiefly covered by ligamentous and bony matter.

When a bone has sustained an injury so as to cause a slight superficial exfoliation, this is generally quickly thrown off, but when necrosis of half the circumference, or even of the whole thickness of the shaft of a long bone, takes place, inflammation and suppuration to a greater or less extent ensue, and new bone is thrown out, which encloses the dead or dying bone. During the time these fragments are being detached, the patients are more exposed to the absorption of pus, and consequently death from pyemia.

The following preparations, Nos. 2934 and 2935, and also that of Private Hunter, from India, are excellent examples of necrosis following these injuries, especially No. 2934, where nearly the whole of the shaft of the bone is dead, and enclosed in a new osseous case. It appears to have been the result of a severe injury to the bone, but without producing a complete fracture.

No. 2934 (see Plate VII., Fig. 2). Femur presenting necrosis of its shaft. The sequestrum comprehends the entire thickness and nearly the whole length of the shaft, and is very rough on the surface. It is detached, and surrounded by a thick uneven shell of new bone, abundantly pierced by cloacæ, so as to expose the dead part extensively. From a man admitted with a gunshot wound of two years' standing; the ball had lodged, but had been cut out a month afterwards. On admission there were two openings between the hamstrings; his general health was very bad, and he died after ten weeks' treatment.

No. 2935. Lower half of the femur, exhibiting necrosis of the anterior circumference of its shaft. The sequestrum is rough on the surface, and loosely contained in a cavity, formed by an abundant deposit of new bone, which is pierced by numerous foramina. From a gunshot injury.

The preparation, No. 2941, shows a gunshot fracture of the lower third of the femur, which is fractured obliquely, and comminuted; a portion is driven into the medullary canal. The margin of both fragments shows the action of the absorbents; there is a line marking the portion of bone in process of separation, and partly necrosed along the margin of the fracture. Secondary amputation was performed at the upper third.

The preparation No. 2931 is an example of a round leaden bullet, producing an oblique fracture through the great trochanter, and becoming firmly imbedded in the cancellous structure of this tuberosity.

An illustration of a grape-shot lodging in bone without splintering, or even causing a fissure, is No. 2932 (see Plate VIII., Fig. 2), where there is a cavity at the base of the great trochanter, containing a grape-shot which is quite loose, the cavity being considerably larger than the ball.

Fracture of the Tibia only.

Gunshot fractures of the leg are frequently of such a severe character as to require immediate amputation, generally in the *thigh*, especially if produced by round-shot or shell. Those caused by musket ball seldom call for the removal of the limb. In the leg, all the detached fragments of broken bone being so near the surface, are easily removed, and irregular portions from both ends of the fractured bone are generally taken away by the saw, if necessary.

When one bone only is fractured, the sound one retains the other in its place, and makes the case much less serious. When the tibia is fractured high up, and the knee-joint has been injured, it will be a case for amputation, as it is only on very rare occasions that the limb can be saved. When the fracture takes place near the ankle, and a fissure extends into the joint, it is rarely that the patient recovers. This, however, took place in Patrick Burrowes, 5th Regt., under partial fracture, page 63.

Under this head 6 have been admitted, of whom 1 has been sent to modified duty, and 5 invalided. Only 1 was produced by grape, and the remainder by musket-ball; 3 were still unhealed. They were all very severe compound comminuted fractures of this bone, and, with the exception of one, all were followed by necrosis to a greater or less extent; 3 occurred in the upper third of the bone, and 3 in the lower, one of which was so close to the ankle-joint that partial anchylosis resulted. One man, of the Royal Artillery, died at Gravesend, but his name is not included in this return, although I take the opportunity of giving the details of the case.

The following is a case of extensive necrosis of the tibia:—

64th Regt.—Private Edwin Beardsall, wounded July 16, 1857, at Cawnpore, by a grape-shot on the right leg, about three inches above the ankle-joint. There was only a slight wound of the skin, but there was a comminuted fracture of the tibia; since then several very large pieces of necrosed bone have come away.

April, 1858. There is now a large deep hollow on the anterior and inner side of the tibia, with two sinuses leading inwards, but no bone could be detected in this direction. There is a third sinus on the inner side of the tibia, where bare bone can be felt. He cannot bear much weight upon the limb, and the ankle-joint is stiff for want of use.

December 22, 1858. Unfit for service; invalided.

The next case is a fracture of tibia, followed by anchylosis of the ankle-joint.

60th Rifles (1st Battalion).—John Flynn, aged 21, wounded at Delhi, June 19, 1857, by a musket-ball, which entered the inner side of the left tibia, two inches above the ankle-joint, and probably passed out at the external malleolus. Several pieces of bone came away from the entrance wound.

July 20th. Wound healed, skin adherent to tibia, ankle-joint partially anchylosed.

The following fatal case is an example of an extensive comminuted fracture which had united, but the bone became diseased:—Royal Artillery.—Gunner John Abberley. This man was admitted into hospital at Gravesend, being unable to proceed to Chatham with the remainder of the men. He was wounded by a musket-ball at Lucknow, the ball striking the upper third of the bone, under the attachment of the ligamentum patellæ, and carrying away a large portion of the bone. When taken on board ship, the wound was said to be about the size of a five-shilling piece, with the bone exposed in the centre, but looking healthy. Gangrene made its appearance about three weeks after sailing. When disembarked, the whole of the soft parts of the anterior surface of the leg between the wounded part and the ankle was one large slough, coming away with the dressings. The whole bone was exposed, the soft part on each side sloughy, blackened, and that offensive smell peculiar to the disease was present. Was emaciated in the extreme, and only kept up by the administration of stimulants to the hour of his death, which took place July 3, 1858.

Post-mortem.—Body.—Much emaciated. *Thorax.*—Old pleuritic adhesions between costal pleura and left lung; both lungs healthy and crepitant; heart and pericardium healthy. *Abdomen.*—Liver healthy; stomach and intestines healthy, as also the remaining viscera. No. 3628. Right tibia, showing a compound comminuted fracture at its upper third, two inches below the tubercle; the fractured ends have become re-united by very abundant depositions of new bone, especially on the posterior surface. In front there is a deep carious cavity, about two inches in diameter, and the same extent in depth. There is one large splinter on the inner side, which has become perfectly united to both ends of the tibia. In the recent state the whole of the anterior surface of the tibia was exposed, and in most part denuded of periosteum.

No. 2947 (see Plate VII., Fig. 4) is an example of a gunshot fracture of the head of the tibia by a musket-ball, making its exit on the inner side of the leg, fracturing and comminuting the bone, but not injuring the joint. The fractured portions have re-united, there is a very abundant deposition of new bone around them, and there is a large cavity in the centre, which is in an ulcerated state. Taken from Private Henry Farrer, aged 32, 34th Regt., an Englishman, by trade a moulder. Total service, fourteen and a half years, chiefly at home, and in the Mediterranean. Always enjoyed good health, and when admitted was a strong-looking man. He was wounded on June 7, 1855, by a musket-ball striking the head of the left tibia, making its exit on the inner side of the leg, fracturing and comminuting the bone, but not injuring the joint. Since then he has always been in hospital. Considerable quantities of bone have come away, but without any severe pain or loss of health. On admission three openings existed, through each of which part of a large sequestrum could be felt with a probe. December 13, 1858.—Died, nearly six months after the receipt of the wound, from pyemia. *Post-mortem Examination.*—*Abdomen.*—A portion of the convex surface of the liver adhered very firmly to the diaphragm by recently effused lymph. Corresponding to this portion, on making a section of the liver, a large diffused abscess was found, which contained ten ounces of pus, which was infiltrated throughout this part of the structure of the liver, several bands of which stretched across the sac. There was no defined wall to the abscess, which appeared to have resulted from the coalescing of several minute abscesses. The sac, on being opened, allowed a large quantity of very fetid gas to escape (sulphuretted hydrogen). There was a second abscess situated to the right of the other, and of nearly the same size. The rest of the structure of the liver was soft and friable, and easily broken up. Weight of liver, 5 lbs. 3 oz.

After a minute and careful examination, and tracing the veins of the left leg through the abdomen, no sign of inflammation could be detected. It is, nevertheless, the opinion of some pathologists, that in the great majority of cases some trace of inflammation in the veins may be found, and when they cannot, the veins affected are supposed to be so small or so obscure that they are overlooked. Further, that pus globules have been detected in the blood of the pyemic, and even in the blood of animals which have died from the effects of pus injected into the veins. The globules of pus have only once been discovered, so that pus globules seem in a great majority of cases to be rapidly destroyed after entering the circulation. This throws considerable doubt on the view that the pus globules become arrested in the capillaries in consequence of their size, and thus establish numerous foci of inflammation. Rokitansky also expresses his opinion very strongly against it. He considers that pyemia occurs not uncommonly as a primitive affection, that is to say, that pus is actually formed in the blood itself in consequence of certain changes of a chemico-vital nature. This is well seen in globular vegetations in the heart. This supposition accounts for cases occasionally occurring in which there are multiple abscesses, yet no source of purulent infection can be discovered.—*Donor, Dr. Williamson, Staff-Surgeon.*

No. 2946 shows the tibia much enlarged, and presenting a cavity in its substance, from which a sequestrum has been detached, with several cloacæ. From a case of gunshot injury.

The preparation, No. 2949, shows a gunshot fracture of the upper third of the tibia. The bone was comminuted, and the fracture united, but with some displacement. A portion of the crest of the bone appears to have been on the point of being necrosed. The external margin of the centre of the fibula is carious.

Fracture of the Fibula only.

4 fractures of the fibula were admitted, of which 3 have been sent to duty, and 1 invalided. 1 only was caused by grape-shot, and 3 by musket-ball. All were healed on arrival.

Fracture of the Tibia and Fibula.

2 have been admitted, and been invalided. 1 was by a musket-ball, followed by sloughing and necrosis. The other was by a grape-shot at the lower third of the leg, followed by anchylosis of the ankle-joint.

75th Regt.—Private Thomas Dabney, aged 38, wounded at Delhi, June 8, 1857, by a grape-shot which struck him on the inner and posterior aspect of the tibia, one inch above the right ankle, and passed out through the external malleolus. Several pieces of bone have come away.

July 20th. Wound healed. Skin adherent to bone, and parts much thickened. Ankle-joint anchylosed. Considerable loss of bone of both tibia and fibula.

November 11, 1858. Invalided.

Preparation No. 2950 is a good example of fracture of both tibia and fibula at the upper third from gunshot. The fractured ends are united by a very abundant deposition of osseous matter, more particularly the tibia, in which there are several cloacæ leading into a cavity in the centre of the bone, where there were some portions necrosed. The fibula has been fractured obliquely; the superior portion lies to the outer side, and overlaps the lower to the extent of an inch, and the latter is united to the tibia by a quantity of new bone. New osseous matter is also deposited to a considerable extent on the surface of the tibia and fibula. On the anterior surface of the tibia, immediately above the fracture, absorption of the new bony matter seems to have been going on.

Necrosis of portions of the shaft of the tibia frequently follows gunshot wounds of the leg,—more rarely of the whole thickness or length of the bone,—leaving sinuses discharging pus for months or years, and rendering the patient liable to death from pyemia, as in the case of No. 2947, Private Farrer.

No. 2946. Tibia much thickened, and presenting a cavity in its surface, from which a sequestrum has been detached with several cloacæ. From a gunshot injury.

The case of Beardsall is also a good example of loss of a great portion of this bone by necrosis.

Division 5.—*Penetrating, perforating, or lacerating the several Structures of the Tarsus and Metatarsus.*

13 were admitted under this head, of whom 4 have been sent to duty, 2 to modified duty, 5 invalided, and 2 remain. 11 were produced by musket-ball, and 1 by round-shot; only one remained unhealed. Two went through the calcaneum; one across the fleshy part of the sole of the foot; two through the tarsus only. The one by round-shot bruised the bones, but did not break the skin, and caused severe injuries to both the tarsus and metatarsus. In those cases that were invalided the bones had been fractured, and tendons and ligaments lacerated, so as to produce in some cases considerable contraction and loss of power in the foot.

The following is an example of this injury:—

24th Regt.—Private Wm. Alexander, aged 21, wounded at Jehlum, July 7, 1857, by a musket-ball, which struck the outer side of the right calcaneum, passed through this bone, and made its exit on the inner side. On September 26, 1857, an incision was made on the posterior part of the os calcis, and necrosed portions of bone were removed, saving the attachment of the tendo Achillis.

August 2, 1858. Wounds healed, but cannot bear his weight on the heel.

August 3, 1858. Invalided.

Class X.—Gunshot Wounds, with direct penetration or perforation of the larger Joints.

This class is restricted to those cases where there is undoubted evidence of the joint having been directly penetrated. For instance, cases of partial or complete fracture of a bone close to a joint are either placed in Class IX., Division 2, or in Class IX., Division 4, according as the case may be. These cases, although generally very severe, and followed by acute inflammation and suppuration, ending in anchylosis (as in the case of Farraher, page 84), are not of such a dangerous nature as when the ball has passed directly through the joint, fracturing the bone, as in those included under the present head.

Admitted from India:—Wounds of larger joints, with fracture of bones, 8; ditto without fracture, 1. Total, 9.

Of these, 6 have been invalided, and 3 remain undisposed of. 1 occurred in the shoulder-joint, 4 in the elbow, 1 in the carpus, two in the knee, and 1 in the ankle. 8 were caused by musket-ball, and 1 by a pistol-bullet. Except 2, all were healed.

In addition to these wounds of the larger joints, there are 3 cases of excision, viz.:—2 of the elbow and 1 of the shoulder-joint, which will be detailed under that head.

In the Crimean War 121 cases occurred amongst the men, of whom 25 died without any operative interference, and 10 among the officers, of which 4 were treated without operation; and of this number, 3 terminated unfavourably[a].

Shoulder-Joint.—Only one case is returned under this head as having arrived from India, and the history of the case is detailed under the class Resections, this operation having been performed at Fort Pitt. In several cases inflammation had taken place contiguous to the joint, resulting in thickening and contraction of the muscular and ligamentous structures, and in some cases the joint had become completely anchylosed, as in Private J. Day, 32nd Regt., under the head of Amputation of the Arm.

The preparations Nos. 2921 and 2922 show the starred fracture and fissures resulting from gunshot injury of the head of the humerus.

"Of 17 gunshot injuries of the shoulder-joint amongst the Crimean wounded, 2 were fatal in the primary hospitals without operation, the cases having apparently been complicated with some injury to the contents of the chest. One patient died in the secondary hospital at Balaklava, of idiopathic fever, contracted while under treatment for the wound, while the whole number of the remaining cases, viz., 14, required operative interference."

Elbow-Joint.—Four cases were admitted from India. All have been invalided.

In these elbow-joint cases, there can be no doubt of the

[a] *Vide* Report on the Crimean Wounded, vol. ii. p. 350.

direct penetration of the joint, with comminution of bone, resulting in anchylosis. In three of them the ulnar nerve was injured. In these instances the olecranon was fractured, and in one case the external condyle; the joint was anchylosed in all of them. In three of them the forearm was at an obtuse angle. In the fourth case the arm was quite straight, and the elbow-joint anchylosed, rendering the arm very useless; but in this case the humerus had also been fractured, making it very difficult to treat. Even now the limb is much more useful than any artificial arm which he could have been supplied with.

In none of them had resection been performed, and it becomes a question whether these patients would have had a more useful arm had the joint been excised, so as to allow of free motion of the joint. If it were possible to induce patients to use the arm at an earlier period of the treatment, they might preserve some motion in the joint.

"Of 30 injuries in the elbow-joint among the men in the Crimean War, and 4 among the officers, 4 were fatal without operation. 2 of these were complicated, with injury of the artery (1 of the brachial and 1 of the ulnar), and the fatal result seems to have been mainly due to the continued effects of shock and loss of blood."

In the two following cases from India, the joint is anchylosed, and the arm in a bent position.

32nd Regt.—Private Harry Arthurs, aged 33, wounded September 27, 1857, at Lucknow, in the left elbow. The musket-ball entered over the external condyle, and passed out on the inner side of the olecranon opening into the joint; severe inflammation and suppuration followed. The arm is now in a bent position, and the elbow-joint is anchylosed. He has lost the power over the fingers, and has no feeling in half of the ring finger and little finger.

June 22, 1858. Invalided.

78th Regt.—Private Wm. Wardleworth, aged 34, wounded at Lucknow, September 25, 1858, by a musket-ball in the right elbow-joint. It entered over the olecranon, and was cut out at the same place the following day; abscesses formed around the joint. 2nd. By a musket-ball on the inner side of the left knee; a flesh wound.

July 13th. The wounds are all healed, and the elbow-joint anchylosed. There is one large cicatrix on the inner side, adherent

August 5, 1858. Invalided.

In the next case the joint was anchylosed, and there was also an injury of the ulnar nerve.

52nd Regt.—Private James Marshall, aged 27, wounded at Delhi, Sept. 14, 1857, by a pistol-ball, which passed through the elbow-joint. It entered close to the outer side of the olecranon process, and between it and the external condyle, and passed through the olecranon, and made its exit on the inner side of this process, close to the ulnar nerve. There was a discharge of synovia from the wound for some days.

July 20th. Wound healed; elbow-joint bent and anchylosed. Has lost the sensation of the little and one-half of ring fingers.

July 22, 1858. Invalided.

The following is a case of wound of the joint, complicated with fracture of the shaft of the humerus. Elbow-joint anchylosed, and the arm in a straight position.

61st Regt.—Private M. Dunne, aged 38, wounded at Delhi, July 9, 1857, by a musket-ball, which entered through the centre of the right deltoid muscle, and passed downwards, fracturing the humerus about its centre, and made its exit at the elbow-joint, where it also appears to have wounded the joint and fractured the olecranon process of the ulna. The arm was placed upon a straight splint. Both apertures of entrance and exit soon healed, but considerable inflammation of the arm and elbow-joint ensued, which was relieved by free incisions.

Sept. 5, 1858. Wounds made by musket-ball healed. There are two sinuses on the outer aspect of the arm, about its centre, leading down to necrosed bone. The fracture at this point is united; the forearm is in a straight position, and the elbow-joint anchylosed. The arm is about 1½ inches shorter than the other.

Jan. 13, 1859. Invalided.

Hip-Joint.—No case of wound of this joint arrived from India. There is a preparation in the Museum, No. 2930, where the old ball is firmly lodged in the head of the femur, having produced only a fissure. This would have been a favourable case for resection. The following is a description of it:—

No. 2930 (see Plate VIII., Fig. 3).—A matchlock-ball, firmly lodged in the head of the femur. The ball entered opposite to the trochanter major, and passed through the brim of the acetabulum. From Private Alexander M'Phail, aged 33, wounded at Dubha, March 24, 1843, by a matchlock-ball, which entered a little above the great trochanter of the right limb anteriorly, and was lost. The leg became powerless. On coming to Colaba, on April 28, he did not complain of much pain, ex-

Fig. 1.

2931

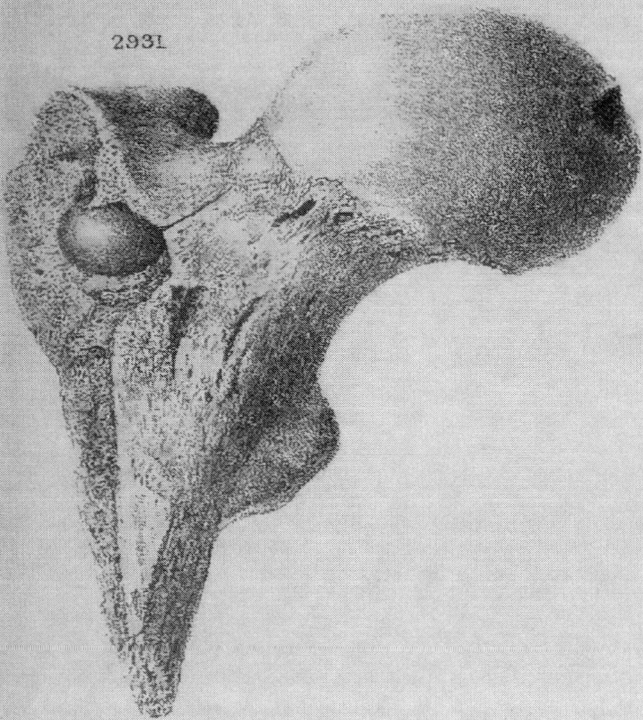

Fig. 2.

2932

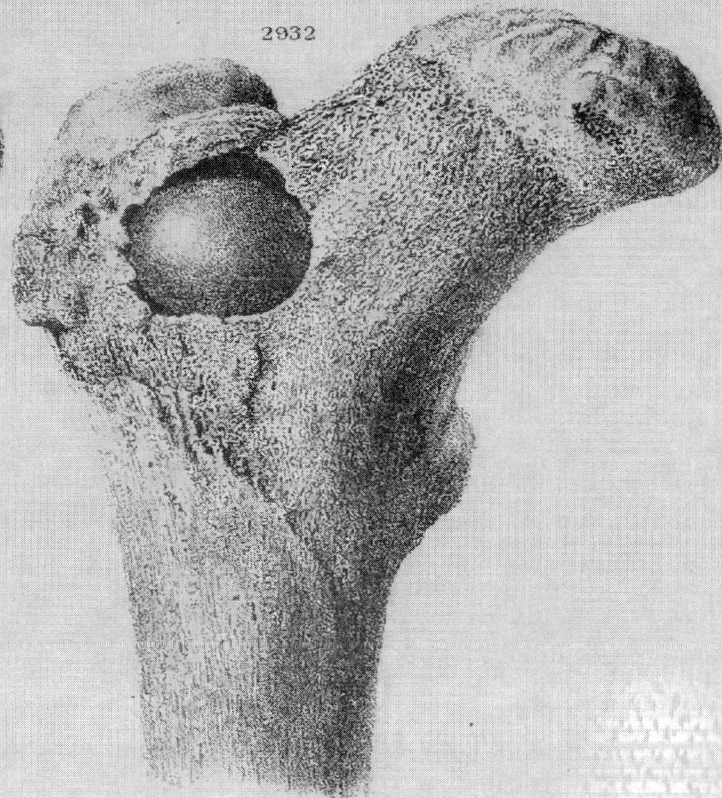

Fig. 4

2933

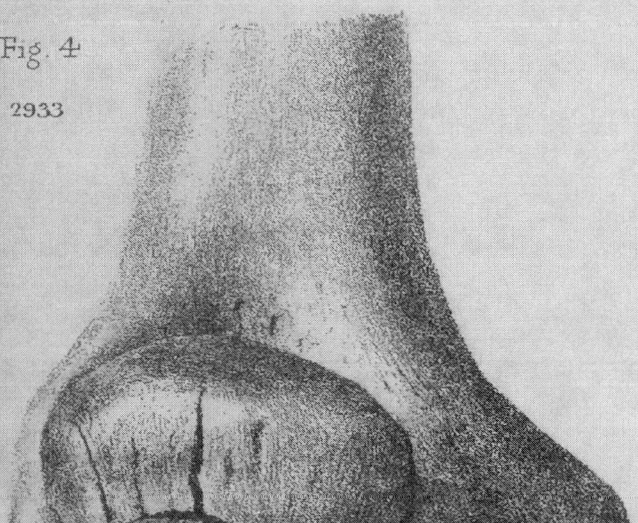

Fig. 3.

2930

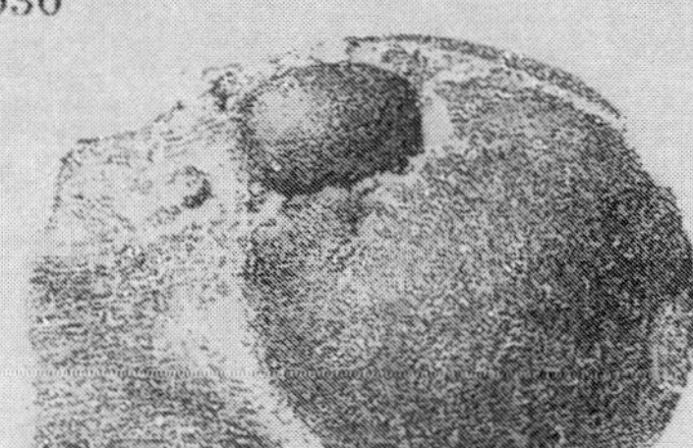

G. H Ford.

W. West imp.

cept when the joint was moved. Slight fulness over the hip was the only symptom of injury. Leeches and counter-irritation were employed, and he seemed to get better. On May 6th he was attacked with trismus, and died on the 9th.

The ball was found imbedded in the head of the femur, which, with half of the brim of the acetabulum, was shattered, and the capsular ligament formed the sac of an abscess, which contained a considerable quantity of pus and spiculæ of bone. The orifice of the wound, it is added, had closed some time previous to his death.

10 cases of wounds of the hip-joint are returned in the Report on Crimean Wounded. In 3 there had been such extensive injury inflicted that they proved fatal in a few hours. 7 were discharged for operation, 1 of which was for amputation at the hip-joint, in a case of extensive longitudinal fracture into the joint; the remaining 6 for resection of the head of the bone.

Excision of the hip-joint for gunshot injury has been performed eleven times. Of these, but one recovered, that of a soldier wounded by a shell at Sebastopol, and operated upon by Dr. O'Leary. The patient was 25 years of age; the head, neck, and trochanter of the femur were removed.

Of the 11 cases recorded, 6 occurred in the Crimean War. 1 occurred in the Schleswig Holstein War; 1 by Dr. Ross, 1 by Oppenheim, 1 by M. Seutin, and 1 by Schwartz. In the Crimean war, excision of the head of the femur was performed six times, and all but one were primary operations. One of the patients survived the operation, and recovered, viz., Private Thomas M'Kenna, 68th Regt. On his arrival at Chatham, the limb is reported to have been about 2½ inches shorter than the other, and capable of bearing some considerable portion of the weight of the body. He could swing it and advance it, but the knee could not be bent. Rotation was admitted to a very limited extent, but performed with considerable pain. The wound was soundly healed, and the man was discharged from the service.

So far as the results of the Crimean war go, it clearly proves the superiority of excision of the head of the femur over amputation at the hip-joint.

The head of the femur has frequently been excised for morbus coxæ, and with great success, but no comparison can be made between it and that for gunshot wounds. No doubt in any future campaign, excision of the hip-joint will be much more frequently employed, and great attention paid to the selection of cases.

Knee-Joint.—2 were admitted from India. 1 was invalided, and the other remains.

In one case the synovial membrane was directly perforated, but no fracture of bone had taken place. In the other it is doubtful if the ball penetrated the cavity of the joint, although the surgeon says it passed through the joint.

In the Crimean war, 23 cases are returned among the men, and 6 in officers. 6 of these patients died, viz., 3 men and 3 officers. 13 men and 2 officers were discharged for operation, but one only of those for resection of the joint, and in that case the operation was a secondary one, an attempt having been made in the first instance to save the limb. In the remainder amputation was resorted to.

In the following case from India, the ball seems to have passed through the condyles of the femur, and was followed by partial anchylosis.

Private John Dunlay, aged 26, wounded at Lucknow, November 16, 1857, by a musket-ball, which struck him on the inner side of the right knee, two inches from the side of the patella, passed through the condyle of the femur and knee-joint, and passed out on the outside of the joint, close to the head of the fibula.

July 13th. Wounds healed, knee-joint slightly bent, and partially anchylosed. Can walk tolerably well, and has a very useful limb; neither cicatrix adherent to the bone.

In the next case it is rather doubtful whether there was direct penetration of the joint.

93rd Regt.—Sergt. David Simm, wounded at Royah, on April 15, 1858, by a bullet which entered 1½ inches to the inner side of the patella, over the innercondyle of the femur, and made its exit at a little higher level, over the tendon of the inner hamstring. It is doubtful if it entered the cavity of the joint, although the surgeon says, "passed through the joint." It was followed by acute inflammation of the joint, and the limb cannot now be fully straightened, and on flexing it a grating sensation is felt.

The following case, although not included in the Return as a wound of the joint, is interesting as showing the inflammation extending to the structures of the joint, terminating in anchylosis.

61st Regt.—Private Martin Farraher, wounded August 25, 1857, by a musket-ball, which entered the external condyle of the left knee-joint, making its exit through the outer side of the popliteal space. Considerable inflammation and swelling of the joint ensued.

Pl. IX.

Fig. 3.

408

Fig. 2.

Fig. 1.

2916

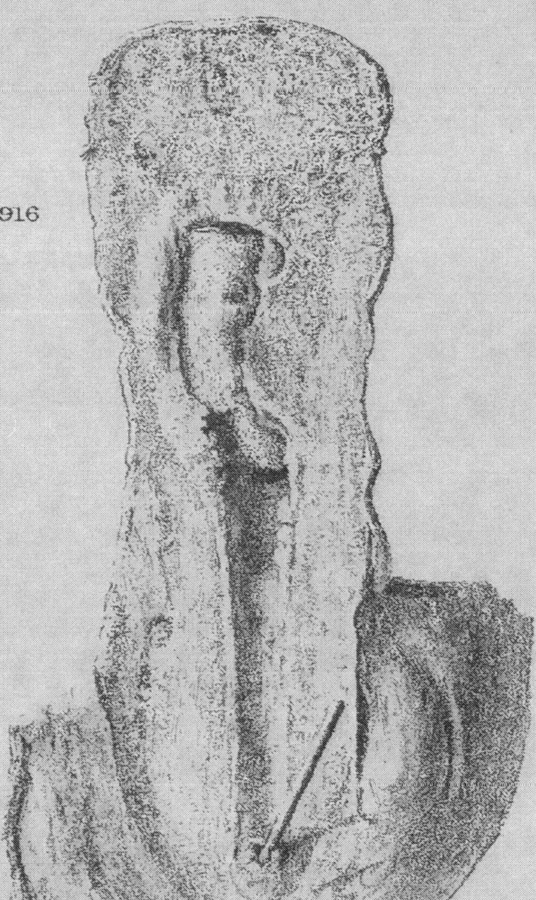

2944

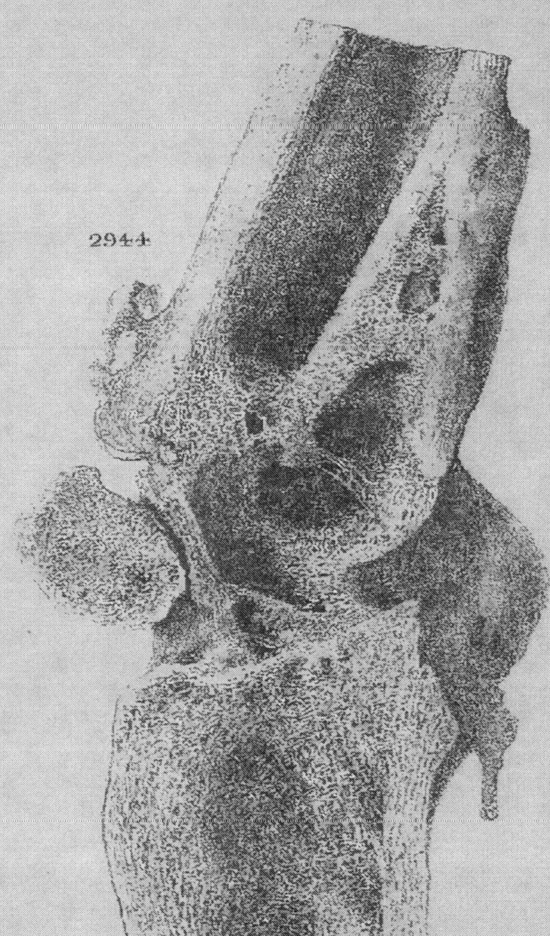

Fig. 3a. Aperture between femoral artery & vein.
b. Coagula in femoral artery & vein.

G. H. Ford. W. West imp.

Sept. 5th The joint itself does not appear to have been wounded, but from its proximity, severe inflammation followed, resulting in complete anchylosis. There are livid spots on his leg, from his constitution being tainted with scurvy, and his gums are spongy.

As yet our experience of excision of the knee-joint in cases of gunshot fractures is not extensive, and the means necessary for after-treatment in military practice are not encouraging, but the success which has followed it in cases of disease of the joint makes military surgeons also wish to extend it to the field. The absolute rest and quiet after the operation which are so difficult to obtain with an army in the field is the chief and the only objection to its adoption.

There are 2 cases recorded of excision of this joint for gunshot injuries--1 in the Schleswig Holstein war, and the other in the Crimean war. Both died.

The following preparation, No. 2933 (see Plate VIII., Fig. 4), shows the condyles of the femur and the patella fractured by a carbine-ball, which in its entrance has comminuted the point of the patella, split the bone longitudinally, and lodged in the bone between the condyles, and caused a fissure through the internal one. From Private M. Walsh, 3rd Light Dragoons. The injury took place while the leg was in a state of flexion, from the accidental discharge of his comrade's carbine. The limb was amputated twenty-four hours after, and the man arrived at Fort Pitt quite well at the end of three months.

The two following preparations, Nos. 2943 and 2944, are very interesting, as showing a perforating gunshot wound through the knee-joint. The ball entered the back part of the joint, and passed directly forwards, and shattered the patella in its exit, followed by recovery and anchylosis. Twenty-six months after the injury the man died at Fort Pitt, of an enormous abscess of the liver, the result of previous service in India. No. 2943. Section of a knee-joint, the bones of which are completely anchylosed, and the capsule obliterated. Dense cellular tissue occupies the interspaces of the articular surfaces. No. 2944 (see Plate IX., Fig. 4). Section of preceding knee-joint, in which the soft parts have been removed, showing the cancelli of the femur and tibia, and also of the patella, completely continuous. The patella was irregularly fractured, and the fragments are now consolidated by osseous matter, and united to the femur. From Private Edward Marr, aged 35. 20th Regt.—Was sent home from India in consequence of a gunshot wound of the left knee-joint, received on Oct. 21, 1833. Admitted into Fort Pitt,

May 10, 1835. Left knee-joint was anchylosed; there was a cicatrix between the vastus externus and triceps, and another immediately above the superior border of the patella. Muscles of the limb much attenuated. General health very indifferent, being under treatment for disease of the liver, of which he died on May 20, 1835.

On post-mortem examination there was found a large abscess in the right lobe of the liver, which communicated through the diaphragm with the base of the right lung. The sac of the abscess contained six pints of thick pus. The spleen was very much enlarged and softened. The peritoneal cavity contained two pints of turbid serum, with flakes of lymph floating in it.

The following preparation of a severe comminuted fracture of the head of the tibia is interesting as showing the discovery of a second fracture of the tibia, not compound, however, and situated about the middle of the bone. The skin over it showed not the least trace of injury from the fracture. How the fracture was produced is a matter for conjecture. If excision of the joint had been contemplated, this after discovery would have been, at the least, embarrassing. No. 2948. Compound comminuted fracture of the head of the left tibia, caused by a shell. There is a second fracture situated about the middle of the bone. From Private James Aitkin, aged 27, who received a severe shell wound of the left leg in the trenches on August 18, 1855. He was standing erect at the time. The knee-joint was distinctly opened into, and the head of the tibia severely comminuted. Amputation was immediately performed, and the patient recovered.—*Donor, Dr. Cowan, Assist. Surgeon, 55th Regt.*

The following preparation shows a bayonet wound of the knee-joint, followed by severe inflammation, profuse purulent discharge, and irritative fever, rendering amputation necessary sixty days after the injury. No. 3633. A portion of quill passed through the original wound shows the direction it took; it is situated just beneath the level of the patella, and a little to the right side. The synovial membrane is thick and gelatinous. From Private John Gannell, West York Rifle Regt., of strong, healthy aspect. While drinking in a public-house, on February 5, 1858, a sergeant of another regiment drew his bayonet and wounded him on the left knee. The wound had every appearance of having penetrated the joint; the pain was excessive; the wound, though small, was deep, and situated just beneath the level of the patella, and a little to the right side of it. Late in the evening of the 5th he was delirious, and in great agony; the pulse alternately full and bounding, and rapid and depressed:

his sufferings were so great that anodynes had to be largely given before anything like a quiet state could be arrived at; the knee became swollen, and the pain continued, and showed signs of the formation of pus in the joint; abscesses also formed outside the joint, and were opened. A profuse discharge of purulent matter continued from the wound, and the man's appearance, pulse, &c., assumed the hectic character rendering amputation of the limb necessary, which was performed April 6, 1858, and the patient recovered.—*Donor, Assistant-Surgeon Taylor, Royal Artillery.*

Ankle-Joint.—The following case was the only admission from India under this head:—

37th Regt.—Private Charles Smith, wounded April 17, 1858, near Azinghar, by a musket-ball, which entered the left instep in front, and above the internal malleolus, and was cut out about two and a half inches lower down, and a little posteriorly. The inner malleolus appears to have been removed subsequently in fragments; anchylosis of the ankle-joint has followed; the foot turns slightly inwards, and the great toe is stiff. Invalided February 9, 1859.

DIVISION 11[a].—*Gunshot Injury of the larger Arteries, not being at the same time cases of Compound Fracture.*

Under this head none were admitted from India. It is, however, probable that the case of Private Bulger, which is detailed at page 61, is of this nature.

It is seldom that primary hemorrhage occurs on the field of battle, even though the ball may have passed directly through the course of a large artery. This is in some measure accounted for, although not entirely, by the round form and the strong elastic coats, but especially by the mobility of the vessel.

Arteries and veins firmly bound to bone are more likely to be injured than those that are lying loose in the fleshy parts of a limb: for instance, the femoral on the brim of the pelvis.

The coats of the veins being thinner than the artery, are much more readily injured, and primary hemorrhage proceeds more frequently from them than from the arteries.

Only 14 such are returned amongst the men during the whole period of the Crimean war, and one in an officer.

The following preparation is a beautiful example of the

[a] This class was left out in the Return of the Wounded from India, in consequence of none having been admitted; but it is inserted here, and thus alters the numbering of the succeeding classes.

elasticity and toughness of the coats of both artery and vein, and likewise of the mobility of these vessels, allowing of being pushed aside by the ball.

No. 408 (see Plate IX., Fig. 3). Portion of the femoral artery and vein, between which a ball has passed, causing mortification of the limb, and death.—*Donor, J. Guthrie, Esq., D. I. G.* This specimen was taken from Private P. Tumbrill, of the Grenadiers of the 74th Regiment, of good stature, who was wounded on April 10, 1814, by a musket-ball, passing from the inside to the outside of the middle of the thigh; he says it bled considerably at first, but the bleeding soon ceased; the wound was not painful, and he thinks he observed the leg and foot to be colder than the rest of his body for the first two or three days, but did not much attend to it, further than conceiving the numbness, coldness, and impeded power of motion as natural to the wound.

"On the 18th April the gentleman in charge of this patient pointed him out to me as an extraordinary case of gangrene, coming on without, as he supposed, any sufficient cause. The wound on the outside of the thigh, or the exit of the ball, was nearly healed, and that on the inside was without inflammation or tumefaction, and with merely a little hardness to be felt on pressing. The pulsation of the artery could be distinctly felt to the edge of the wound; the leg was warm; the gangrene confined to the toes; the artery of the other thigh could be distinctly traced down to the tendon of the triceps. As he was at a small hospital about two miles from town, I did not see him again until the 20th, and afterwards on the 23rd, when, although the gangrenous portion included all the toes, it had the appearance of having ceased. Satisfied that it would again extend, I left directions with the assistant surgeon, that the limb should be amputated below the knee.

"The surgeon, whom I had not seen, and who did not understand the subject, disobeyed the order, conceiving there must be some mistake. On visiting the hospital a little after daylight on the 25th, I was greatly annoyed at finding the operation had not been done, and that the mortification had begun to spread the evening before. It was then too late; on the 26th it was above the ankle, with considerable swelling up to the knee; at night the man died, and the next morning at six o'clock I removed the femoral artery from Poupart's ligament to its passage through the triceps, which part was affected by the mortification.

"The ball had passed between the artery and vein in the spot where the vein is situated nearly behind it, and adherent only by cellular membrane, through which the ball made its passage; the coats of the vein being little injured, and those of the artery not destroyed in substance, although bruised; it was at this spot much contracted in size, and filled above and below by coagula, which prevented the transmission of blood, and the vein above and below the wound was filled with coagulum, and was also impassable."

This preparation is unique. It is perhaps the only one in existence proving the elasticity which vessels possess, and their capability of avoiding to a certain extent an injury about to be inflicted on them.

Ligature of Arteries.—2 cases requiring ligature of arteries occurred: 1 was deligation of the radial artery, eleven days after a gunshot fracture of the ulna, implicating this artery; the other was for secondary hemorrhage, one month after a gunshot wound of the leg, with partial fracture of the tibia; the ligature was placed upon the lower third of the posterior tibial. In a third case it is stated that the brachial artery was tied, but there appears to be some doubt on the subject. The following is one of the cases:—

53rd Regt.—Private Patrick Hanafin, wounded at Lucknow, November 16, 1857, by a musket-ball, which entered on the inner side of the left tibia, about three inches above the ankle-joint, and passed through the fibula, three inches from its lower extremity; about one month after, secondary hemorrhage took place, following sloughing of the wound, requiring ligature of the posterior tibial at the lower third of the leg. He was also wounded in the right thigh by a musket-ball, which entered on the outside near its centre, and passed through in front of the femur, on the inner side, close to the course of the femoral artery.

Both wounds are healed.

Class 12.—Gunshot Wounds, with direct injury of the large Nerves, not being at the same time Cases of Compound Fracture.

6 cases have been admitted, 3 invalided, and 3 remain. All were wounds of the brachial plexus. In one there was complete paralysis of the arm, with a partial fracture of the scapula. In two the paralysis was only partial. In one case the arm hung powerless by the patient's side, without the slightest sensation or power of motion, and the temperature much diminished. In the other two cases the impaired condition of their arms, although not to such a great extent, was yet very nearly so. Various treatment was adopted,—blisters,

galvanism, friction, cold and salt-water baths, &c., without the slightest benefit.

Large nerves, like arteries, generally escape being wounded by musket-balls. When they are injured, paralysis of the limb, to a greater or less extent, comes on, along with numbness and wasting of the muscles of the extremity, as occurred in the following cases:—

Private Peter Clear, wounded at Cawnpore, November 28, 1857, by a musket-ball, which entered the posterior part of right shoulder, above the spine of the scapula, and caused a partial fracture of this bone, and passed directly forwards, and was cut out immediately above the centre of the right clavicle.

August 16, 1858. Wound healed. He has entirely lost the sense of feeling and of motion in this arm, which hangs quite powerless by his side. Temperature diminished, and the integuments are bedewed with a cold, clammy perspiration.

November 23, 1858. Invalided.

78th Regt.—Private John Daniels; wounded at Lucknow by a musket-ball, which entered below the right scapula, and passed out about two inches further forward; re-entered in the axilla, and came out about the middle of the inner edge of the deltoid. He was shot from behind while loading his firelock.

July 13th. Wounds healed. Loss of sensation and motion in arm, which is always covered with perspiration.

August 5th, 1858. Invalided.

CLASS 13.—SWORD AND LANCE WOUNDS.

Under this head 12 have been admitted, of which 5 have been sent to duty, 1 to modified duty, and 6 invalided. In 2 cases the elbow-joint was wounded; in 5 the forearm; in 2 the back of the wrist: and in 3 cases the fingers and thumbs were injured. In the 6 invalided the condition of the forearm and fingers was more or less injured. In 1 of them both bones of the forearm were severed, with nearly total loss of use of the hand resulting. In another the tendons of the ring-finger of the right hand were cut, and the joint became anchylosed; and in the third there was impaired use of the thumb and index-finger from the extensor tendons having been cut.

In the case sent to modified duty the elbow-joint had been opened into, followed by anchylosis. There is also a second case of anchylosis of the elbow-joint that has been invalided.

90th Regt.—Private Joseph Albison, wounded by sabre-cut on the posterior part of the right forearm, about 3 inches above the wrist, which nearly severed both bones. There is now loss of power of the extensor muscles; there is considerable deposition of new osseous matter around the cut bone. The hand is slightly bent inwards, powerless, and he cannot use his fingers, which are in a straight position.

June 15, 1858. Invalided.

9th Lancers.—Private Joseph Twining, wounded at Delhi by a sabre cut on the posterior and under surface of the left elbow-joint, which appears to have cut the external condyle of the humerus and olecranon. No pieces of bone came away, and the wound did not heal completely for three months.

August 2nd. Wound healed. Elbow-joint in a bent position, and completely anchylosed. Cannot pronate and supinate the hand.

September 3, 1858. Sent to modified duty.

Class 14.—Bayonet Wounds.

Only 2 cases of this description of injury are returned as having arrived from India. One was a wound in the back, close to the spinous processes, and he was sent to duty; and the other was in the forearm; and, from the man's account, the ulnar artery was wounded, and tied at the wound of entrance.

The following preparation of a bayonet wound of the brain through the orbital plate of the frontal bone ought to have been placed under "Sabre or Bayonet Wounds of the Head" (page 19):—

No. 2792. Left orbit, exhibiting a small punctured fracture of the orbital plate of the frontal bone, just above the os unguis; the margins of the fracture are driven inwards. This was produced by an accidental wound from a bayonet. The wound in the skin was very small, and soon healed, but the patient had pain in the head, fever, then coma, and death on the twelfth day after the injury. A small triangular portion of the fracture was elevated inwards and sticking in the dura mater, and the membranes of the brain were inflamed near the wound, and covered with puriform matter.—*Donor, Dr. Young, Surgeon, 95th Regiment.*

Class 15.—Miscellaneous Wounds and Injuries received in Action.

9 have been admitted, of which 2 have been sent to duty, 1 to modified duty, and 1 invalided. 3 were caused by explosion of gunpowder, producing severe burns, and 1 by a fall

from a ladder at Lucknow when examining a mine belonging to the enemy, injuring his leg. One had lost his ear, and another an eye.

Balls, Missiles, &c.—No. 2952. Specimen of the matchlock-ball used by the inhabitants of the Euzuffii country in the Himalayas, extracted from a wound received in action.—*Donor, Dr. Jephson, A. S., 9th Lancers.*

No. 2953. Rifle-ball which was lodged near the hip-joint from a Malay of Ceylon Rifle Regiment. Result, abscess and death.—*Donor, Mr. Swettenham, A. S. S.*

No. 2957. Grape-shot, weight 6 oz., from the thigh of Sergeant Brown, 14th Regt., invalided for shortening and much impaired use of left leg, after gunshot compound comminuted fracture of the left thigh at the siege of Sebastopol.—*Donor, J. R. Taylor, C.B., D. I. G.*

No. 2958. Cast of a ball. This grape-shot fractured the alveolar process of the superior maxillary bone, and passed downwards, and lodged in the right side of the neck, having fractured the lower jaw, a portion of which was extracted with some of the teeth. The ball weighed 1 lb. 3½ oz., and was removed by a careful dissection, as it was lying close to the carotid. He still complains of slight pain when pressure is made on the lower jaw, and he can only make use of liquid diet. —*Donor, Dr. Dartnell, D. I. G.*

No. 2951. Three pieces of coin removed from the thigh. "A Hanoverian soldier received a severe wound from a grape-shot which struck him on the external part of the thigh, producing very extensive laceration. On the second day he was brought to hospital, and the usual dressings applied. On the fifth day a long, narrow passage was discovered by the probe, seeming to run nearly the whole length of the vastus externus muscle. On cutting into this, three pieces of coin (which, from the very curious way in which they were compacted, I thought worthy of being presented to the Director-General of Hospitals) were extracted from the parts.

"This poor fellow, a raw recruit, had no money whatever about him, nor even a pocket to contain it, and fervently protested against his right to this forced loan. He accounted for it by supposing it was carried from the pocket of his comrade, who stood before him in the ranks, and who was killed by the same shot.

"The coins, consisting of two five-franc pieces, were obviously first struck by the shot, and carried along by it. For nearly one half of their surfaces the silver pieces adhered closely together; on the other, where the ball had struck their edges, the metal was flattened out, and somewhat hollowed. In this hollow lay the copper coin, in some degree adapted to the shape of the depression in the larger pieces.

"I cannot omit noticing here a trait strongly illustrative of the mobility of mind which characterizes soldiers, and their proneness to superstition and belief in omens, which a surgeon acquainted with their character may often turn to their benefit.

"The part of these two coins which had been flattened out happened to be that on which Napoleon's head was impressed. From one it was nearly effaced, and on observing this circumstance to the patient and his comrades, an universal burst of joy echoed through the ward. The young Hanoverian exulted in the share he conceived he personally had of contributing to the downfall of the French Emperor. His health rapidly improved, and I have no doubt this simple circumstance had a good effect upon every man who witnessed it."—*Donor, Dr. Guthrie, D. I. G.*

AMPUTATIONS.

Total number of amputations, 158. Of these, 3 have been sent to duty; 21 to modified duty; 123 invalided; 2 died; and 9 remain undisposed of.

It may be mentioned that Mr. Heather Bigg supplied the men with every mechanical appliance, on the most approved principle which his experience could suggest.

Amputation at the Shoulder-Joint.—6 have been admitted and invalided; only 1 remained unhealed. 4 were by the superior and inferior flap; and 2 by the anterior and posterior flaps; the stumps were all good and round, and the integuments not puckered; both methods of operating gave equally good results: all were done under the influence of chloroform; all were primary operations.

In the following case the stump sloughed.

Rifles (2nd Battalion).—Private James Gayler, wounded at Cawnpore, November 28, 1857, by a grape-shot, which shattered the arm. Amputation was performed at the shoulder-joint, three hours after the injury, under the influence of chloroform, by anterior and posterior flaps; the ligature did not come away for some time, and caused considerable irritation; sloughing also took place, with much suppuration.

July 11, 1858. The stump is good and solid, although there are three small portions of the margins of the flaps unhealed, with exuberant granulations arising from them.

September 3, 1858. Modified duty.

The two following preparations are good examples of necrosis affecting the stump of the humerus, comprising nearly the entire thickness of the shaft, occurring in a very scrofulous subject, and which demanded secondary amputation at the shoulder-joint, two years after the primary operation. Death from pyemia ten days after the last operation. No. 2916 (see Plate IX., Fig. 2). Section of the stump (in spirits) of the upper half of the humerus, removed by secondary amputation at the shoulder-joint. A portion of the upper part of the shaft of the bone, immediately below the neck, about two and a half inches in length, and comprising nearly the entire thickness of the shaft of the humerus, is necrosed; the necrosed portion is firmly enclosed in a case of new bony deposit, through which there are two apertures opening externally; the medullary membrane is soft, spongy, and inflamed; the medullary canal is open inferiorly at the amputated extremity, and allowed of the free escape of discharge; a thick layer of new bone entirely surrounds the whole of the shaft. No. 2917. Is a section (dry preparation) of the preceding. The entire shaft of the bone, with the exception of its neck, is surrounded by a thick, granular deposit of new bone. The compact structure of the old bone is soft and cellular; the medullary canal is also rough and spongy, the result of inflammation of its lining membrane; there is also an aperture in the neck of the bone, communicating with the medullary canal.—*Donor, Dr. Dane, Staff-Surgeon.* This specimen was taken from Private James Clarke, 77th Regiment, aged 21, of highly strumous diathesis and unhealthy aspect. He had suffered amputation of the arm about the middle third, in May, 1854, in consequence of severe gunshot wound, and, on admission into hospital at Colchester, September 4, 1855, the wound was healed through the greater part of its extent, but there were two small sinuses opening on the face of the stump, which discharged profusely, and dead bone could be detected by a probe through each of them; his appetite was bad, and general health indifferent.

April 19, 1856. His progress was so unsatisfactory that the operation of removing the stump, at the shoulder-joint, was decided upon, as the only chance of saving his life. He was low after the operation, but rallied, and seemed likely to do well, until the 23rd, when he became low, irritable, and unable to take nourishment; constant nausea and diarrhœa set in, and a train of inflammatory symptoms, under which he gradually sank, and died on May 1, 1856.

At the post-mortem examination, the liver was found large and friable; the right kidney diseased; serous effusion in the peritoneal cavity and deposits, marking the existence of sub-acute peritonitis; and the intestines were soft, dark, and injected. The whole structures around the shoulder-joint were abnormal and degenerated; and the clavicle, scapula, and first rib extensively affected with disease, similar to that exhibited in the preparation of the humerus. The cancellous structure appeared disorganized, dark, spongy, and soft, and filled with a dark brown fluid (which was not found in the humerus when removed), in which it appears that the bony structure was gradually becoming, as it were, dissolved, but there was no attempt at formation of new bone around, as in the arm.

The two succeeding preparations from two soldiers of the same regiment, who received compound comminuted fracture of both bones of the forearm, at Inkerman, November 5, 1854. Amputation at the centre of the arm was immediately performed. Necrosis followed in both cases, and amputation at the shoulder-joint was performed on both patients, July 25, 1855, eight months after the primary operations.

The necrosis in the preceding preparation, No. 2916, and the two under notice, appears to have originated in inflammation of the medullary membrane and canal.

No. 2918. The necrosed portion comprises the entire thickness of the end of the shaft, and is about five inches in length, nearly detached, and partly surrounded by a new osseous case. From Private James Leman.—*Donor, Dr. Browne, Assistant-Surgeon, Coldstream Guards.*

No. 2919. The necrosed portion comprises the entire thickness of the shaft, and is about two inches in length, and is not situated at the end of the stump, but at the upper part of the shaft, close to the tubercle, and is partly surrounded by new osseous matter. From James Curds.—*Donor, Dr. Munro, Surgeon-Major, Coldstream Guards.*

Amputation of the Arm.—46 cases have been admitted, of which 3 have been sent to modified duty; 40 invalided; 1 died; and 2 remain undisposed of. Of these, 33 were in the middle of the arm, and 12 in the upper third; 1 quite close to the tubercle; 41 were healed, and 5 still remain open; in 37 instances the cicatrix did not adhere to the bone; and in 9 cases it was found to adhere to a greater or less extent, generally very slightly.

In 36 instances the flap operation appears to have been performed, and the circular method 8 times. 30 operations were done under the influence of chloroform, and 14 cases without this agent. 35 were primary, and 11 secondary amputation. In 3 cases severe sloughing of the stump followed.

2 of them ultimately recovered; the third died at Fort Pitt. In 1 case there was also anchylosis of the shoulder-joint, resulting from the injury caused by round-shot.

The following is an example of sloughing taking place in the stump, along with hemorrhage from some small vessel, occurring in a scrofulous subject after a second amputation in the arm. It also shows how difficult it would have been to have found and secured the bleeding vessel in this case.

32nd Regt.—John Healy, aged 20, wounded at Lucknow, September 5, 1857, by a round shot on the right wrist, carrying away the hand. The forearm was amputated the same day by double flaps under chloroform. The stump assumed an unhealthy appearance, and sloughed. One large piece of bone came away. Amputation was a second time performed on board a ship, at the Cape of Good Hope, April 13, 1858, eight months after the accident. The stump has never entirely healed.

Fort Pitt, June 11, 1858. There is now considerable inflammation around the stump, particularly along its inner side, and the cicatrix is raised and œdematous. It is probable that the bone is again diseased. There was thick, purulent discharge from the stump, but he did not complain of pain in it. Appetite impaired, and bowels constipated, he is of a very strumous diathesis. On June 17 matter formed on the inner side of the stump: distinct fluctuation could be felt. On the 23rd, the stump became suddenly very painful, redder, and more tense, and an incision was made into it, from which was discharged dark coagulated blood. He was in a very low, ænemic state. Oozing of blood took place from the stump, which was restrained by the application of ice. He gradually became weaker, and died on June 27th.

Treatment.—Nourishing diet, wine, quina, &c. To the stump, fomentations, poultices, cold applications, and ice, as the state of the case required.

Sectio Cadaveris, twelve hours after death.—*Cranium.*—Brain healthy. *Thorax.*—Heart empty; blood pale, and destitute of red globules; lungs œdematous, but otherwise healthy. *Abdomen.*—Convex surface of the right lobe of the liver adhered to the diaphragm by old bands of adhesion, and a few slight depressions, resembling cicatrices. The other viscera in this cavity were healthy, with the exception of being pale and bloodless; veins healthy.

Stump tense and swollen, with several incisions on its surface, from two of which large coagula projected. The stump was of a very fœtid and gangrenous smell, and on cutting into it a very large cavity was found to extend from the extremity of the bone up along its inner side into the axilla, as far as the first rib, completely dissecting the axillary vessels and nerves, and likewise the muscles of the arm; the shoulder-joint was opened into by absorption of the capsular ligaments, the cartilage covering the head of the bone and glenoid cavity being discoloured by the blood, but not diseased. The vessels from which the blood was poured out could not be detected even by careful dissection, showing how difficult, or almost impossible, it would have been to find the bleeding vessel, or even the axillary itself, in such a case in the living subject. A small portion of the extremity of the amputated humerus was bare and carious, which probably was the origin of the deep-seated inflammation and suppuration, causing ulceration of one of the smaller bloodvessels, and consequent hemorrhage, followed by a gangrenous state of the stump, and death from exhaustion. Preparation No. 3632. Stump of the right humerus after secondary amputation, resulting from a gunshot wound. The end of the bone shows that the medullary canal has not been closed, although nature has attempted to do so to some extent, and the end is partially rounded off; the shaft of the bone is roughened, particularly below the head of the bone, where it is denuded of periosteum, and is carious.

The following case shows anchylosis of the shoulder-joint after amputation of the upper third of the arm:—

32nd Regt.—Private John Day, wounded at Lucknow, August 27, 1857, by a round-shot, which carried away a great portion of the upper arm, shattered the humerus, and left the large vessels and nerves hanging loose. Amputation was performed by the circular method, one hour after, under chloroform, at the upper third, close to the insertion of the deltoid. Exfoliation of the extremity of the bone took place, and it was extracted June 29th.

August 16, 1858. Wound healed; cicatrix adherent to the end of the bone; shoulder-joint anchylosed, the result of the injury and surrounding inflammation.

September 2, 1858. Sent to modified duty.

Amputation of the Forearm.—19 cases were admitted, of which 1 has been sent to modified duty, 17 invalided, and 1 remains undisposed of. All have apparently been performed by double flap. 16 were done under the influence of chloroform; 15 were primary, and 4 secondary amputations; 4 in the upper, 11 in the middle, and 2 in the lower third. All were healed. In no instance was the integument adherent to the bone; the stumps were good.

Amputation of the Thumb.—12 were admitted. 1 has been sent to duty, 5 to modified duty, 5 invalided, and 1 remains undisposed of. All were healed.

Amputation of the Fingers.—38 were admitted, of which 1 has been sent to duty, 10 to modified duty, 26 invalided, and 1 remains undisposed of.

There were several good examples of conservative surgery, where the whole of the hand had been taken away, with the exception of the thumb and forefinger. In many cases, where one or more fingers had been amputated, the others had become so bent and contracted that forcible extension had to be employed, with very good results.

Amputation at the Hip.—The following case is interesting, as being, perhaps, the first successful case of amputation at the hip-joint after a gunshot fracture:—No. 2929. Head of the femur removed by amputation at the hip at Brussels after the battle of Waterloo. The fracture extends obliquely downwards from the neck of the bone through the shaft, leaving the trochanter minor only attached to the head of the femur.—*Donor, Mr. Guthrie, D.I.G.* This specimen was taken from Francois de Gay, Private in the 45th Regiment of French Infantry.—He was wounded at the battle of Waterloo by a musket-ball, which entered behind, fractured the neck of the femur, and made its exit anteriorly, about four inches below the groin. He was admitted into the Elizabeth Hospital, July 5, 1815, much exhausted. In addition to his wounds, which had put on a sloughing appearance, he suffered from an extensive sore on the sacrum, which was caused by lying on the wet ground for five days. Amputation was performed on the 7th, nineteen days after the injury.

In September the wounds were healed, and he was capable of walking three miles at a time, the wooden leg which he had attached to his body being thrown forward by an exertion of the muscles of the trunk. He was placed in the Hotel des Invalides.

Amputation of the Thigh.—11 have been admitted, 9 invalided, 1 died, and 1 remains; 1 only occurred in the upper third, and 10 in the middle third; 1 died. All appeared to have been flap operations, and performed under the influence of chloroform. In 8 instances the integument was not adherent to the bone, and the stumps were very good. In 3 cases the skin adhered very slightly, but the covering was still good. 3 cases remained unhealed. The case at the upper third of the thigh was performed by anterior and posterior flaps, forty-six days after, under chloroform. The wound healed; stump good; and skin not adherent. The stump was so short that it could not be retained in the bucket by any contrivance of Mr. Heather Bigg. In 8 cases amputation was performed from one to twelve hours after the accident; in 1 case from one to two days; in 1 case from three to seven days; in 1 from eight days to one month. 4 were apparently by lateral flaps, and 6 were by the anterior and posterior flaps, and in the other case the mode of operating is not stated.

The following case, from India, is an example of extensive necrosis of the shaft of the stump of the femur, causing death from exhaustion:—

2nd Battalion Rifles.—Private John Sole, aged 24, wounded November 28, 1857, at Cawnpore, on the right leg, by a grapeshot. Amputation was immediately performed at the middle of the thigh. He was admitted into Detachment Hospital, Gravesend, on July 8, 1858, from on board ship. He was much emaciated. The stump had never been properly healed, and on board ship it sloughed. There were several unhealthy-looking sores on the stump along the line of incision, with a profuse discharge. After being in hospital he improved considerably, sores appearing more healthy, and for a time he gained both flesh and strength. He occasionally complains of great pain in the stump, referring it to the end of the bone. About three weeks before his death a swelling of considerable size appeared on the outer surface of the stump, which burst, and a large quantity of unhealthy pus escaped, and dead bone was detected through the newly opened sore. He now began to lose flesh and strength; the discharge increased from all the sores, appetite bad, stomach very irritable, and bed-sores appeared. He died on September 11, 1858.

All the viscera in the different cavities were healthy. The following is a description of the stump of the femur:—Preparation No. 3625. Right femur showing necrosis of the internal layer of the shaft of the bone, the result of amputation, at the middle third, after a gunshot injury. The preparation exhibits the extremity of the stump, where the saw was applied, in a necrosed state; and it shows the smooth surface left by the saw as plainly as when recently done. This portion consists of the entire thickness of the bone; and there is also a mark on its side where the saw had been accidentally applied, and apparently destroyed the periosteum. A thin lamina of necrosed bone extends upwards, to within an inch of the trochanter major lying encased in the old and new shaft. The shaft of the bone has become expanded and opened out in texture, and covered with large irregular nodules of new bone. There are three cloacæ on the anterior surface of the femur, and one three inches in length posteriorly at the linea aspera, through which the necrosed portions can be seen. The extremity of the stump presents a large aperture one inch in diameter, leading into the medullary canal; and through it the necrosed portions can be drawn out. The disease seems to have commenced by inflammation in the medullary membrane, producing necrosis of a thin layer of the shaft. The old shaft still remains, and is covered with new bone, except at the very extremity, where the saw was applied; and it is probable that the scratch made with the saw was the primary cause of the death of the bone, and also of the inflammation of the medullary membrane.

The following is an interesting case in several points of view. It shows a wound of the knee-joint, followed by complete disorganization of its structure, demanding amputation three months after the injury. The stump had nearly healed when he was attacked with acute ostitis; and he died from exhaustion forty-four days after the limb was amputated. No. 2940. Femur showing the results of periostitis following amputation at the lower third of the thigh. Nearly ten inches of the shaft of the bone is either necrosed, or in a dying state, and is partially encased in a new bony shell. It also shows that the periosteum has a large share in the generation of new bone.—*Donor, Dr. Williams, Assistant-Surgeon, Rifle Brigade.* This specimen was taken from Private John Walsend, aged 29. Wounded September 8, 1855, by a bullet through the integument of the knee. There being every probability that the joint was injured, perfect rest was enjoined, and leeches, fomentations, &c., applied. These means were ineffectual for restraining the inflammation. The joint appeared quite disorganized, and constantly discharged purulent matter. Amputation was performed on the 2nd November, 1855. On the 15th the wound had almost healed up, when he was attacked by acute ostitis in the shaft of the bone. The great suffering attending the inflammation wore out his strength, and he died on the 16th December, much exhausted and emaciated.

Amputation of the Leg.—18 have been admitted. 17 have been invalided, and 1 remains undisposed of. 11 were performed at the middle third, 4 at the upper third, and 2 at the lower third. 15 appeared to have been performed by the usual flap operation, but in 2 of them a large anterior flap was also made of integuments, in 1 of which the stump was good, and in the other the skin was adherent. 2 were by the circular method, and in both of them the skin was adheent; but still these two stumps were as good as any of those by the flap. 14 cases were operated upon under the influence of chloroform, and 3 without it. In 8 instances, out of the total 18 cases, were the integuments free, and movable over the crest of the tibia. In 3 cases only were the stumps unhealed. 16 were primary, and 2 secondary amputations.

The following is an interesting example of the foot having been shattered by round-shot, requiring immediate amputation, and where there also existed a simple fracture of the femur of the same thigh, which was not discovered for six weeks after.

78th Regiment.—Private Duncan M'Crea, aged 36, wounded September 24, 1857, at Lucknow, by a round-shot striking the left foot, and carrying it away; at the same time he received an oblique fracture of the lower and middle thirds of the same thigh, which was not detected for six weeks after. The leg was amputated four inches below the knee, by the flap operation, about a quarter of an hour after, under chloroform.

June 11, 1858. There is now a good stump, and the skin does not adhere to the bone. The femur appears to have been fractured obliquely, commencing about four inches above the knee; one extremity of the bone is found to project in front, and a groove is felt to proceed upwards and backwards to the posterior part of the middle of the femur. The knee-joint cannot be completely extended or perfectly flexed, so as to fit a leg stump, in consequence of the contraction of the rectus and vastus muscles. The left femur is an inch and a half shorter than the right, and he states that it only united on the passage home. Invalided August 18, 1858.

One case of amputation at the *ankle-joint* was performed, eight hours after the accident, in the 75th Regiment; and a very good stump resulted.

With regard to the respective merits of the two methods of amputation at the ankle-joint, viz., that recommended by Mr. Syme, and that by Pirogoff, the profession has not yet come to a decision. Still, there appears to be some advantage in the latter, as being easier of execution, giving a longer stump and firmer support. In Pirogoff's operation, when the ends of the tibia and fibula are sawn straight across, there is always great difficulty, or rather almost an impossibility, in bringing the calcaneum into apposition with the end of the tibia; so that it has been found necessary to remove several slices of the calcaneum with a strong bistoury before the bones could be brought to fit properly. To remedy this difficulty, the following modification was adopted in a case operated upon by Staff-Surgeon Dr. Williamson, on the 24th December, 1858, at Fort Pitt.

The articular extremities of the tibia and fibula were sawn off *obliquely*, the thick part of the *wedge-shaped pieces* being *posterior*. The os calcis fitted admirably. The wound healed rapidly, and a very good, solid stump resulted. The sawing of the ends of the bones obliquely is an improvement, and is well worthy of being generally adopted, as allowing of easy adaptation of the calcaneum to the ends of the leg-bones.

Two cases of amputation through the medio-tarsus arrived from India. In one the operation was performed three hours and a half after the injury, caused by a musket-ball through the arch of the foot. In the other the operation was performed twelve days after the accident. In both cases the stumps were good.

EXCISIONS.

3 cases of resection of joints have arrived from India, viz., 1 of the shoulder, and 2 of the elbow-joint.

Out of a total number of 36 primary resections that occurred in the Crimean war—of which 28 were performed on the superior, and 8 on the lower extremity—of the former 6 died, and of the latter 4 died, viz., 4 cases of excision of the head of the femur.

Shoulder-Joint.—Only one case of resection of this joint was admitted from India; but there is another case where a secondary operation was performed at Fort Pitt, in a patient who is returned as a wound of the joint.

In the Crimean war the head of the humerus was removed twice as a primary operation during the first period of the war, or that ending March, 1855, and 8 times during the second. 1 of the two first-mentioned ended in death, and of the 8 subsequent operations only 1 proved fatal.

" The head of the bone was five times removed as a secondary operation, without a single casualty, all the cases except one making good and comparatively rapid recoveries. In addition to these, there was a case in which the head of the bone and a large portion of the scapula, broken into fragments, were removed."

" Out of the total number, then, of 16 cases, 3 deaths took place, or 18·9 per cent. Had this operation not been resorted to, amputation at the shoulder-joint, it is believed, would have become necessary in all."

19 cases of resection occurred during the Schleswig Holstein war. Of these, 7 died, and 12 recovered with useful and movable articulations. Of the 7 fatal cases, 2 were primary operations, 2 were performed during the reaction stage, and 3 were secondary resections.

This mortality at first sight appears rather high; but the

conditions under which they were performed must be taken into consideration: they were done, as Esmarch states, under circumstances in which more than a third of all amputations of the arm died. They died of pyemia. Stromeyer and Esmarch both agree that the most favourable time for resection is either within the first twenty-four hours, or when suppuration is fully established.

Abscesses and sinuses are apt to form in the vicinity of the joint, and occasionally cause considerable trouble. A good deal of this depends upon the form of incision selected, so as to allow of the free discharge of pus. Bandens, who has had great experience, recommends the straight incision, so as to avoid cutting the fibres of the deltoid, and it is also necessary to save the long tendon of the biceps, if possible.

Stromeyer advocates the semicircular incision over the posterior surface of the joint, which certainly allows of the free exit of pus; but to cut across the fibres of the deltoid must in some degree impair the limb, although Esmarch states that to cut across the fibres of the deltoid does not much interfere with its after usefulness. Even in those cases where the single incision has been employed, the patient frequently has very little or no power of raising the arm from the side, as was exemplified in the case of Private James M'Donald, 79th Regiment, from the war in India, and others that have come under notice here.

As there are generally two apertures, the surgeon may wish to include them in his incision; but each method will possibly be found to suit in different cases. It is seldom necessary to take away more than the head and a portion of the shaft—perhaps nearly as low as the insertion of the deltoid; but in the Schleswig Holstein war it is shown that as much as four inches and a half were removed from the humerus, and yet a most useful arm remained.

Esmarch makes the following observation:—"It is curious that the operation on the left side seems to give less favourable results than on the right. 6 of 12 died of those resected on the left; 1 out of 7 of those resected in the shoulder on the right side. A similar proportion held good in resections of the elbow, in whom, of those operated upon on the left, 4 in 19, on the right 2 in 20 resections proved fatal. From this, the fatality attending operations on the left arm to that on the right is as 3 to 1; but of course further observations are required to enable conclusions to be deduced."

The following is a primary case of excision of the head of the humerus by one straight incision, from India:—

Private James M'Donald, 79th Highlanders, wounded at Lucknow, March 11, 1858, by a musket-ball, which struck him in the left shoulder, splintering the head and shaft of the humerus to a considerable extent. The ball then passed backwards and downwards, injuring the lower angle of the scapula, and lodged between that bone and the ribs, from which position it was extracted. The shattered parts of the head of the humerus and part of the shaft were excised the same day, by one long incision through the anterior part of the deltoid muscle.

September 26, 1858. There is a large cicatrix in front of the shoulder-joint, and a sinus in its centre, leading down to diseased bone. He cannot raise the arm from the side, on account of loss of power over the deltoid.

He has been sent to modified duty, December 22, 1858.

The two following cases of secondary operations are good examples of perforating gunshot wounds through the head of the humerus, followed by anchylosis of the joint, and the track of the ball remaining carious, necessitating resection of the head of the bone:—

93rd Regt.—Private John Frazer, aged 33, seventeen years' service. Was wounded at Lucknow, March 14, 1858, by a musket-ball, which entered the left shoulder beneath the acromion, and passed backwards, apparently through the humerus, close to its head.

March 2, 1859. There is now anchylosis of the shoulder-joint. Much dead bone in fragments can be felt both from the anterior and posterior openings. General health good.

17th. The head of the humerus was excised, and it shows the track of the ball to be in a carious state. Numerous smaller pieces were also taken away by the gouge. Invalided.

9th Regt.—Private John Morgan, aged 39. Eighteen years' service, ten of them in India. Was wounded in action at Idaliff, in September, 1842, the ball passing through the right shoulder-joint and injuring the scapula. On admission into Fort Pitt Hospital, June 9, 1844, there were three sinuses, two on the anterior aspect of the joint, one opposite the coracoid process, where the ball entered, and the other at the lower border of the axilla, and another on the posterior aspect, the exit of the ball, each communicating with diseased bone. Excision was performed on June 22, 1844, by Assistant-Surgeon Dr. Williamson; a semilunar flap was made of the deltoid, embracing the entrance and exit of the ball; and on attempting to dislocate the humerus, this was found impossible, on account of complete anchylosis of the joint. The humerus was sawn across about two inches below its head, then cleared of soft parts, and raised; its attachment to the glenoid cavity was broken down by means of cutting pliers. The wound healed quickly, and he gradually regained the power of motion in the arm. No. 2919. Head and neck of the right humerus, which was excised on account of caries consequent on a gunshot wound. The large, deep groove is the track of the ball; it is carious a little below the groove. There is an aperture, about one-fourth of an inch in diameter, situated on the inner aspect of the bone, leading into the medullary cavity. The tubercles and upper part of the shaft are enlarged from depositions of new osseous matter.

Resection of the Shaft of the Humerus.—The following preparation, where three-quarters of an inch of the shaft of the humerus were resected in a case of comminuted fracture eight months after the injury. Death from pyemia one month after the operation. No. 2920. Humerus exhibiting a gunshot fracture below its centre. The end of the lower portion is healthy. There is a superficial exfoliation of a large portion of the outer layer of the shaft of the superior fragment, and also of the medullary canal.—*Donor, C. Reade, Staff Surgeon.* 95th Regt.—Private Thomas, aged twenty-two years, when on duty in the trenches before Sebastopol, was struck by a fragment of shell on the left arm, producing a compound comminuted fracture of the humerus, an inch below its centre, August 18, 1855. On admission into Brompton Hospital, February 18, 1856, the wound had healed, but re-opened on April 18th. At this time firm ligamentous union had taken place between the ends of the fractured bone, and a false joint had been established.

On April 22nd he was in an excellent state of health. It was determined to perform the usual operation for effecting union of the shafts of the bone. A free and deep incision was made in the outer aspect of the left arm, about an inch below the insertion of the deltoid muscle, and carrying it perpendicularly downwards to a level with the condyles, dividing, amongst other muscles, the outer belly of the triceps. Owing to the obliquity of the fracture, and the strength of the ligamentous structure holding the bones together, some difficulty was experienced in passing the knife through the ends of the bones. After further dissection, three-quarters of an inch were sawn off with a metacarpal saw from the fractured ends.

There was but little blood lost during the operation, though several ligatures had to be applied. The patient was under the influence of chloroform. Some considerable time after, he was removed to his ward, and reaction had taken place;

profuse hemorrhage occurred from the wound, probably from deeply seated muscular branches, but was stopped eventually by the application of ice. The limb was placed in a gutta-percha splint. On the evening of the following day the patient was feverish, with hot and dry skin, quick pulse, flushed face, and great thirst. He went on favourably till the 27th, when he had an attack of what is described as intermittent fever. On the 30th he was improving in health, the wound contracting and granulating. Discharge profuse, but healthy. On the 1st, 2nd, and 3rd May he was slightly delirious, and so restless that the limb was constantly disturbed. On the 4th severe dyspnœa came on. The wound still continued to contract, and the discharge was healthy. On the 8th he had a slight attack of shivering. All the ligatures came away. Continued to gain strength up to the 17th. His appetite was enormous; bilious vomiting came on, owing, as was supposed, to the mixture of some incompatible articles of extra diet. On the 19th he passed a restless night. The vomiting stopped, but there was a good deal of nausea. Had a severe attack of dyspnœa, with short cough, and symptoms of congested lungs, especially of the left. Tongue furred; discharge from the wound less. The cough and dyspnœa more severe, and the heart's action very rapid. These symptoms continued to increase, especially those of pericardial effusion, and he died on May 21st.

Sectio Cadaveris, thirty-three hours after death.—Pericardium contained two pints of turbid serum, and was coated with a thick layer of recent effused lymph of a granular appearance, with several patches of vascularity. Valves healthy; both lungs congested; liver healthy. An abscess was found in the external margin of the spleen. *Left Kidney.*—There was an abscess, about the size of a walnut, on its upper and inner surface, immediately below the capsule. There was also a similar abscess in the right kidney. Stomach and intestines healthy; veins not examined.

In the case of Major M., recorded under the head of "Fracture of the Humerus," resection may also ultimately be required.

Elbow-Joint.—Two cases of excision of this joint arrived from India, and are interesting. In one there had also been a fracture of the humerus, and the arm is now in an extended position, and the motion of the elbow-joint is very limited; in the other, the arm hangs powerless by the side, like a flail, without strength to raise the forearm, and he can only move the thumb and fingers slightly; it is so useless and cumbersome, that he has frequently requested me to amputate the arm; this has not been done, because, when he keeps the arm in a sling, he has still the use of the fingers and thumb. In this case a very large extent of the ends of the bones of the elbow-joint must have been removed, and also the tubercle of the radius, with the attachment of the biceps; the distance between the bones is very great, and there does not appear to be ligamentous matter effused between the bones. The man himself, when out of hospital, does not use the sling; consequently, the arm is so much in his way that he fell down when under the influence of liquor, and injured it very much. In both these cases the operation was performed by the H incision.

The extent of the articular ends of the bones that can be removed, compatible with a useful limb, should be such as to allow of free motion between the ends of the bones, so that there can be no fear of their becoming jammed. It appears that about one inch or one inch and a half, of all the three bones composing the joint, should be always about the extent removed.

When only a small extent of the articular ends of the bones is removed, anchylosis is almost certain to be the result, from the extremities of the bones becoming jammed, and preventing free motion even from the first.

Partial resection of the shoulder and elbow-joints does not permit of nearly so much motion as where the entire articular surfaces are removed, and they generally terminate in partial or complete anchylosis, as occurred in a case on which I operated lately; and there is one arrived from India, where the joint is anchylosed, with the arm in a straight position, and hanging quite useless by the side, but, as already stated, there was also a fracture of the humerus in this instance.

In all cases of gunshot wounds of the elbow and shoulder-joints, where there is direct injury of the capsule, with fracture or splintering of the bones forming the articulation, primary resection should, as a rule, be performed on every occasion, as being more certain to terminate in a speedy cure, and to leave a much more useful limb, with a good artificial joint, than where the case is left to nature, when the track of the ball and joint itself generally become carious, and continue to discharge for years, ultimately requiring resection to be performed.

The cases of Frazer and Morgan are examples of the above remark in reference to the shoulder-joint; and there are several cases of wounds in the elbow and shoulder-joints from India where complete anchylosis has taken place, and which would have much more useful limbs had excision been performed with the usual amount of success.

5th Regt.—Private Thomas Johnstone, aged 30, wounded at Mussleagh, by a sword-cut in five different places, March 19, 1858. One wound opened freely into the right elbow-joint, and severely wounded the radius and humerus, necessitating excision, by the H incision, of this joint, which was performed two days after; this had been deferred until then, on account of the movements of the forces. Another shot carried away the left thumb, which was amputated.

September 26th. The arm hung powerless by his side, and he has not the power of raising the forearm; he can use his fingers; the ulnar nerve seems to have been injured, as he has not the feeling of the ring and little fingers; when his arm is supported in a sling he will still have a useful forearm. Invalided, December 29, 1858.

75th Regt.—Sergeant John M'Donald, aged 26, wounded at Delhi, June 15, 1857, by a musket-ball, in the posterior part of the left elbow-joint. Excision, by H incision, of the fractured parts was immediately performed, and several pieces of bone came away at the time, and several pieces came away afterwards.

July 20, 1858. Wound healed; arm in an extended position, and can be only slightly bent; he cannot open the little and ring fingers, and the others are also powerless. The arm is about three inches shorter than the right. September 8, 1858, sent to modified duty.

In the Crimean war "22 operations in all were done on the elbow-joint, of which 3 ended fatally, and 2 more deaths took place after secondary amputation; in all a total of 5 deaths, or 22 per cent. of the cases treated. This per-centage slightly exceeds that of resection of the shoulder-joint, but in both instances resection afforded a much more favourable result as to the mortality, than amputation."

In the following case, on which I recently operated on account of disease,—and where I took away the whole of the ulna, two inches of the humerus, and the head and neck of the radius close to the tubercle,—the man can now (four months after the operation) bend his forearm, raise his hand behind his head, and lift a twenty-eight pound weight from the ground; he can also pronate and supinate the hand; there is no anchylosis of the wrist-joint, and he can use his fingers well.

This case also shows the large amount of bone which can be removed from the upper extremity compatible with the patient regaining a very useful arm and hand; and although not resulting from a gunshot wound, still it appears of sufficient interest to be given here.

Pl. X.

Fig. 2.

Fig. 1.

3636

G.H Ford. W West imp.

Staff Armourer Sergeant H. W., aged 26, two years and a half in the service, of which five months were in China. He is of healthy appearance. Was admitted into the general hospital, Hong Kong, in August, 1857, immediately after his arrival from England, with symptoms of acute hepatitis and pleuritis. Active depletion was had recourse to, and calomel and opium administered, which produced salivation, and the disease was arrested; on the 3rd September a large phlegmonoid tumour was found near the elbow-joint, which was opened, and a large quantity of matter evacuated. From that time the ulna became permanently enlarged, extensive necrosis took place, and a few spiculæ of bone came away. He was admitted into Fort Pitt Hospital on the 1st of August, 1858, with numerous sinuses along the inner side of the left ulna, extending down to the diseased bone, and the probe also entered from behind into the elbow-joint. The disease in the ulna was imagined to terminate about an inch above the wrist, but to extend into the elbow-joint. The radius did not appear to be engaged in the disease. The patient's general health was good.

August 30th. The whole of the ulna, as well as an inch and a half of the extremity of the humerus, and also the head and neck of the radius, were removed by a single incision along the posterior and inner side of the forearm by Staff-Surgeon Dr. Williamson. The skin was dissected back, and the ulnar nerve cleared away from the internal condyle. The disease was found to extend the entire length of the ulna. An endeavour was at first made to disarticulate at the wrist by cutting the lower attachments of the ulna; but it was found to be much more easily accomplished by cutting the triceps and lateral ligaments, and getting into the elbow-joint. The entire ulna was now disarticulated and dissected out. An inch and a half of the ends of the humerus and radius were then removed. No vessels required to be tied. The wound was left open for three hours, when sutures were inserted, and the arm placed upon a straight splint.

September 1st. The arm was placed in a semi-bent position, and laid upon a gutta-percha splint.

5th. The whole of the wound had healed by the first intention, and the sutures were removed.

8th. The splint was taken away, and he could move his fingers and hand, and get his left hand to the mouth with the assistance of the right, but could not do so of his own accord.

10th. The wound completely healed twelve days after the operation.

12th. He continues to move the joint and use his finger;

but is only just able at present to raise the forearm, showing that he is beginning to regain the power over the biceps muscle. The arm is, however, small and weak. There is every prospect of the patient having a very useful arm and hand. His general health is good, and he is out of bed, and going about.

No. 3636 (see Plate X., Fig. 1).—On examination of the parts removed, it was found that the whole of the ulna was much enlarged, from deposition of new osseous matter, enclosing several portions of necrosed bone. The whole of the cartilages covering the ends of the bones forming the elbow-joint were absorbed, and the bones carious.

It is not often that a case occurs where the disease is entirely confined to the ulna and bones of the elbow-joint. With regard to the operation, it was found much more easy to disarticulate from the elbow than from the lower extremity of the ulna, and care was required to avoid cutting the arteries and nerves by keeping close to the bone. It is also worthy of remark that no vessel required to be tied, although they must have been increased in size to supply the enlarged ulna. The rapidity with which the wound healed is also remarkable.

The following is a case of partial excision of the wrist-joint:—

78th Regt.—Corporal David Fotheringham, wounded July 12, 1857, by a musket-ball in the right wrist-joint. The ball entered on the anterior surface, and passed directly out on the posterior. Several small pieces of bone were taken away at the time. The hand has been kept in a straight splint ever since, and he has now nearly lost the use of the fingers. The wrist-joint is much enlarged; the aperture of entrance of ball is long since healed,—that of exit still remains open; diseased bone can be felt.

May 10, 1858. Diseased bone taken away by the gouge.

June 2nd. Invalided. General anchylosis of the carpal bones. Wound nearly healed; has the use of the fingers to some extent.

Note.—Post-mortem appearances, furnished by Mr. Birkett, in the case of Private James Beahan, who was admitted into Guy's Hospital, December, 1858, and died February 13, 1859, whose case is noticed at page 42.

"The peritoneum and the abdominal viscera were healthy, except adhesions between the spleen and left kidney and colon. In the left loin a fistulous opening led directly into the descending colon; it passed immediately below the lower edge of the left kidney. A sinus extended downwards behind the left colon, as far as the ilium. A small piece of lead was fixed in the capsule of the spleen, but gave rise to no disease. Parts of the two lowest left ribs were necrosed. The lumbar vertebræ were slightly curved to the right side. A hole, with smooth edges, was seen between the left transverse processes of the second and third lumbar vertebræ. It corresponded to the inter-vertebral foramen, but was larger than natural, and admitted the finger into the vertebral canal. From this hole the bullet had, doubtless, made its exit into the colon. It was difficult to find the point of entrance of the ball, as the original wound had healed, and the tissues around were much indurated. The cicatrix in the skin of the lumbar region was seated a little to the right of the spinous process of the fourth lumbar vertebra; and on dissecting down to the arches, it was evident that the ball had entered between the arches of the third and fourth lumbar vertebræ, fracturing their arches, and, passing along the third lumbar, made its exit between the tranverse process of the second and third. The arches of the third and fourth lumbar vertebræ, which had probably been broken, were now anchylosed."

"It will be remembered that the ball struck him whilst he was crawling along the ground, and it took an upward direction. It entered to the right side of the spinous process of the fourth lumbar vertebra, passed behind the body of the third lumbar and the spinal cord, and, emerging between the transverse process of the second and third lumbar on the left side, entered the left or descending colon, and was voided per anum.

"For some weeks after the injury fæcal matter passed by the primary wound, but at last this entirely healed. For a few weeks, although suffering pain, he was free from any fæcal fistula. An abscess then formed in the left loin, which broke, and continued open to the end. Through this, fæces continually passed. Both kidneys were very large, white, and granular. The connective tissue of the body generally was infiltrated with serum."

It is curious to remark the numbers that are wounded, and the proportion that survive under the different classes of gunshot wounds. Take, for example, the total number of cases that arrived from India under wounds of the three large cavities:—

Head, 15, or 2·48 per cent. of the total that arrived, viz., 603. Chest, 19, or 3·16 per cent. Abdomen, 8, or 1·15 per cent.

The numbers from India do not represent the frequency or

the mortality of gunshot wounds in those different regions; but from April 1, 1855, to the end of the Crimean war,[a] the total wounded was 7153. Of these, in the—

Head, 851 treated, or 11·9 per cent. of the entire wounded; 170 died, or 20 per cent. of those treated. Chest, 420 treated, or 5·8 per cent. of the entire wounded; 118 died, or 28·1 per cent. of those treated. Abdomen, 235 treated, or 3.28 per cent. of the entire wounded; 131 died, or 55·7 per cent. of those treated.

From this, it would appear that gunshot wounds of the head (in siege operations, at least) are twice as frequent as those of the chest, and more than three times compared to the abdomen; while wounds of the chest are more than 8 per cent. more fatal than the same injury in the head; and gunshot wounds of the abdomen are 27 per cent. more fatal compared to those of the chest.

On comparing the frequency among the cases from India of—

Gunshot wounds of the superior extremity, 159, or 26·36 per cent. of the total that arrived. Amputation of the superior extremity, 127, or 21·22 per cent. Total, 286, or 47·42 per cent.

Gunshot wounds of inferior extremity, 162, or 27·03 per cent. Amputation of the inferior extremity, 34, or 5·80 per cent. Total, 196, or 30·84 per cent.

From this it is seen that there is only an excess of 3 in the wounds of the lower over that of the upper extremity; but the proportion of successful amputations is very much in favour of the superior extremity, there being 83 more than in the lower extremity. The number of amputations of the arm are 46, and of the thigh, 11. This difference is to be attributed to the greater mortality in amputation of the thigh over that in the arm. The amputations of the forearm and leg are very nearly the same, being 19 of the former, and 18 of the latter. There are 53 amputations of the fingers and thumbs, while there are only 2 of the toes; still, these minor operations raise the proportion of the total number of successful amputations of the superior over the inferior extremity.

In the Crimean war there were—

Gunshot wounds of the superior extremity, 2083 treated, or 30·2 per cent. of the entire wounded; 47 died, or 2·9 per cent. of those treated. Gunshot wounds of the lower extremity, 2198 treated, or 31·76 per cent. of the entire wounded; 166 died, or 8·3 per cent. of those treated.

Had the result of the operations performed been added, the difference would have been increased in a very material degree.

[a] Vide Report.

The number of cases that occurred under the remainder of the classes is very small, as the following extract from the return of the India cases will show :—

Gunshot wounds of the face, 22, or 3·64 per cent. of the entire wounded.

Ditto, neck, 7, or 1·15 per cent.

Ditto, back and spine, 9, or 1·49 per cent.

Ditto, perineum, genital and urinary organs, 3, or 0·49 per cent.

Ditto, with direct penetration of the larger joints, 8, or 1·32 per cent.

Ditto, with direct injury of the large arteries, not being at the same time cases of compound fracture, 0.

Ditto, with direct injury of the larger nerves, not being at the same time cases of compound fracture, 6, or 0·99 per cent.

Sword and lance wounds, 12, or 1·99 per cent.

Bayonet wounds, 2, or 0·33 per cent.

Miscellaneous injuries received in action, 9, or 1·49 per cent.

On referring to the "Return of the Wounded from the Crimean War," nearly the same proportion under these classes is found to hold good :—

Gunshot wounds of the face, 533 treated, or 7·45 per cent. of the entire wounded; 14 died, or 2·60 per cent. of those treated.

Neck, 128 treated, or 1·79 per cent. of the entire wounded; 4 died, or 3·12 per cent. of those treated.

Back and spine, 326 treated, or 4·55 per cent. of the entire wounded; 45 died, or 13·49 per cent. of those treated.

Perineum, genital and urinary organs, 55 treated, or 0·76 per cent. of the entire wounded; 17 died, or 30·96 per cent. of those treated.

With direct penetration or perforation of the larger joints, 121 treated, or 1·65 per cent. of the entire wounded; 25 died, or 20·66 per cent. of those treated.

With direct injury of the larger arteries, 12 treated, or 0·16 per cent. of the total wounded; 8 died, or 66·66 per cent. of those treated.

With direct injury of the larger nerves, 22 treated, or 0·30 per cent. of the total wounded; 8 died, or 36·36 per cent. of those treated.

Sword and lance wounds, 7 treated, or 0·09 per cent. of the total wounded; 1 died, or 14·28 per cent. of those treated.

Bayonet wounds, 36 treated, or 0·50 per cent. of the total wounded; 4 died, or 11·11 per cent. of those treated.

Miscellaneous wounds received in action, 126 treated, or 1·62 per cent. of the total wounded; 6 died, or 4·76 per cent. of those treated.

RETURN OF CASES *landed at Gravesend from the* 31*st March*, 1859, *to* 30*th June*, 1859.

Classification and Specification of Wounds and Injuries.	Landed at Gravesend.	Discharged to Duty.	Discharged to Modified Duty.	Invalided.	Died.	Remaining undisposed.
1. Gunshot Wounds of the Head:—						
1. Contusions and simple flesh-wounds.						
2. With contusion or fracture of the cranium, ...	4	2	. .	2		
3. With depression, or displacement of both tables, ...	2	. .	. .	2		
Total, . . .	6	2	. .	4		
2. Gunshot Wounds of the Face:—						
2. Penetrating, perforating, or lacerating the bony structures, without lesion of important organs, ...	1	1				
3. Gunshot Wounds of the Neck:—						
1. Simple flesh contusions and wounds, .	1	1				
4. Gunshot Wounds of the Chest:—						
1. Simple flesh contusious and wounds, .	2	2				
2. With injury of bony or cartilaginous parietes, without lesion of contents, .	1	1				
5. Perforating contents, ...	1	1				
Total, . . .	4	4				
7. Gunshot Wounds and Contusions of the Perineum and Genital Organs, not being at the same time Wounds of the Perineum, .	1	. .	. .	1		
8. Gunshot Wounds of the Upper Extremities:—						
1. Simple flesh contusions and wounds, .	11	5	2	1	. .	3
2. With contusion and partial fracture of long bones, including fracture of the clavicle and scapula, ...	14	4	2	5	. .	3
4. With compound fracture of humerus, .	4	. .	2	1	. .	1
,, ,, radius, . .	1	. .	1			
,, ,, ulna, . .	2	2				
5. Penetrating, perforating, or lacerating the several structures of the carpus and metacarpus,.	2	. .	2			
6. Dividing or lacerating the several structures of the carpus and metacarpus, .	1	1				
Total, . . .	35	12	9	7	. .	7

Classification and Specification of Wounds and Injuries.	Landed at Gravesend.	Discharged to Duty.	Discharged to Modified Duty.	Invalided.	Died.	Remaining undisposed.
9. Gunshot Wounds of the Lower Extremities:—						
1. Simple flesh contusions and wounds, .	22	10	1	3	. .	8
2. With contusion and partial fracture of long bones, or of the bones of the pelvis, in their relation to the lower extremities, ...	14	2	1	3	. .	8
3. With fracture of long bones by contusion from round shot, ...	2	. .	1	1		
4. With compound fracture of femur, . .	4	. .	. .	4		
,, ,, tibia only,	1	. .	. .	1		
5. Penetrating, perforating, or lacerating the several structures of the tarsus and metatarsus, ...	2	1	. .	1		
Total, . . .	45	13	3	13	. .	16
11. Gunshot Wounds with direct penetration or perforation of the larger joints, . . .	2	. .	. .	2		
12. Gunshot Wounds with direct injury of the larger nerves, not being at the same time cases of compound fracture, ...	2	1	. .	. .	.	1
13. Sword and Lance Wounds, ...	23	3	3	8	. .	9
15. Miscellaneous Wounds, ...	2	2				
Total Wounds received in Action, ...	122	39	15	35	. .	33

Return *of Capital Operations.*

Description of Operation.	Landed at Gravesend.	Discharged to Duty.	Discharged to Modified Duty.	Invalided.	Died.	Remaining undisposed.
Amputations.						
Upper extremity.						
Arm, ...	4	. .	. .	4		
Forearm, ...	1	. .	. .	1		
Thumbs, ...	1	. .	1			
Fingers, ...	7	. .	4	2	. .	1
Lower Extremity.						
Thigh, at middle, ...	3	. .	. .	3		
Leg, ...	1	. .	. .	. .	. .	1
Toes, ...	1	. .	1			
Amputations, since March 31, 1859, ...	18	. .	6	10	. .	2

SUMMARY.

	Landed at Gravesend.	Discharged to Duty.	Discharged to Modified Duty.	Invalided.	Died.	Remaining undisposed.
Amputations, since March 31, 1859, ...	18	..	6	10	..	2
Wounded, since March 31, 1859, ...	122	39	15	35	..	33
Total wounded, since March 31, 1859, ...	140	39	21	45	..	35
Total wounded previous to March 31, 1859, .	603	193	67	263	7	73
Total landed at Gravesend, up to June 30, 1859,	743	232	88	308	7	108

It is probable that, for the next twelve months or more, a few men may still be coming home from India, viz., those who were only slightly wounded and had been sent to duty, and subsequently invalided either for the wound or for disease; but nearly all must have now arrived.

The greater number of the cases under the different divisions are of such a slight nature that they do not require notice.

CLASS I.—GUNSHOT WOUNDS OF THE HEAD.

2 cases of depression and displacement of both tables of the skull were invalided, on account of giddiness and inability to stand the heat of the sun.

CLASS IV.—GUNSHOT WOUNDS OF THE CHEST.

There is one case where the ball seems to have hit the sternum and to have dropped off, although the document states that the ball entered the left side, and still remains in the cavity of the chest. Great dyspnœa followed; bubbles of air were forced through the wound, and blood in considerable quantity was brought up by fits of coughing. Has been sent to duty.

In the following case the ball perforated the lung; the patient recovered, and has been sent to duty.

Private Thomas Powell, aged 27, 9th Lancers; was wounded September 14, 1857, by a bullet, which entered the right side of the chest, 1½ inches below the sternal extremity of the clavicle, and passed out over the centre of the body of the right scapula, passing between first and second ribs; several fragments of bone came away from the front wound. The man says violent inflammation of the lungs followed.

June 7, 1859. Wounds soundly healed, but right side hardly expands so much as left; health seems good. Sent to duty.

Class VII.

1 man was admitted under this head. He was wounded on the 13th September, 1857, at Delhi, by a fragment of a shell. The posterior part of the scrotum was torn away, and the testicles, which were laid bare, subsequently sloughed.

April 27, 1859. Complains of pain in back when he walks far, and has difficulty in retaining his urine, especially at night. The right cord can be felt, but ends abruptly. A fragment of the left testicle, about the size of a hazel-nut, can be felt attached to the left cord. Invalided.

Class VIII.—Gunshot Wounds of the Upper Extremities.

The cases of compound fracture of the humerus, of the radius, and of the ulna were soundly healed, and the patients had good useful arms.

Class IX.—Gunshot Wounds of the Lower Extremities.

Division III.—*With Fracture of Long Bones by contusion of Round Shot.*

2 cases of simple fracture of the long bones of the lower extremity were admitted. One man received a contusion from a spent round shot, on the 5th May, 1858, which fractured the lower third of the right femur, but inflicted no wound: a simple fracture. The limb is now quite good, but 1½ inch shorter than its fellow. Invalided April, 1859.

In the other case, a spent cannon-ball struck the right leg, a little above the centre of the right shin, fracturing both tibia and fibula; skin not broken. There is now slight irregularity of the tibia, and the limb is somewhat wasted, but is straight and in a good position. Shortening of limb to the extent of about an inch; rigidity of ankle-joint. Invalided April, 1859.

Division IV.—*Compound comminuted Fractures of the Femur.*

4 cases have been admitted since March, 1859, of which the following are the detailed histories:—

In the first case, it is impossible at the present time, now nineteen months after the injury, for a surgeon to say whether immediate amputation ought to have been performed; but it appears to testify to the great advantages and superiority of the dooley over every other means of conveyance for cases of gunshot fracture of the femur; as there can be no question that this patient could not have survived such repeated removals by any other method of conveyance.

1st Battn. 8th Regt.—Private William Cunningham, aged 31, on the 14th September, 1857, at Delhi, in the trenches, received a gunshot comminuted fracture of the left femur; the ball entered on the outer aspect, some 7½ inches below the trochanter, and has never been found. He states that he was at once placed in a dooley, and the limb shortly after put up in a long splint; was twice moved to different houses which were set apart as hospitals at Delhi, and at the expiration of three months he was sent to Umballa in a dooley, a distance of eleven days' march, without any splint, the bone still ununited; and, according to the patient's statement, the splint never was replaced. The upper fragment of the femur projected in front, and protruded through the integuments, and a portion came away by necrosis; extensive abscesses formed, and the limb was left perfectly free of any apparatus, as the patient was in such a weak and exhausted condition that it was not expected he would survive; and it was thought that he was not capable of bearing amputation of the limb. He states, that while at Umballa the fracture united, and after being there two months he was sent to the Hill Station at Landaur, in a dooley.

Fort Pitt, 27th April, 1859.—The outer fragment projects outwards and forwards, and is covered by integuments; the limb is 4¾ inches shorter than the opposite one; the toes are pointed downwards, and the limb wasted. There is an open sinus at the seat of the fracture, which extends deep below the fragments, although bare bone cannot be felt. The knee-joint is stiff, and the ligamentous structure rigid from want of use; but the leg is in a straight position.

20th May.—The sinus has healed, and the patient can bear his weight upon the limb. He has been fitted with a high-heeled boot with a long thigh-piece, &c., attached, by means of which apparatus he is able to walk tolerably well, with the assistance of a stick. Invalided May, 1859.

53rd Regt.—Private Samuel Shaw, aged 36, was wounded February 3, 1858, near Lucknow, by a musket-ball, which entered the outer side of left thigh, about 4 inches above the knee, fractured the femur, made its exit on the inner side, and then entered the opposite thigh, whence it was removed by incision from near the patella.

May, 1859.—Left thigh 1½ inch shorter than the opposite,

and much atrophied, with two cicatrices adherent to the bone; the wound has only very lately healed, and the knee is stiff; he has a very useful limb, and is able to walk well with a high-heeled shoe. Invalided 13th June, 1859.

1st Battn. 24th Regt.—Private George Williams, aged 29; ten years' service; wounded at Umritzir on the 18th October, 1857, by a musket-ball, which entered the right groin a little external to the vessels, and came out just posterior to the great trochanter, fracturing the femur; many fragments of bone came away from the opening.

June, 1859.—Aperture of entrance and exit healed, but leg shortened $1\frac{1}{2}$ inches; a sinus exists on the outer side of the hip, leading down to diseased bone; has just recovered from an attack of erysipelas of this thigh; the right leg is $1\frac{1}{2}$ inches shortened; there is every prospect of the patient having a very good and useful limb; is able to walk about upon it, with the assistance of a stick. Invalided 29th June, 1859.

86th Regt.—Private J. Curtis, aged 35; fourteen years' service; wounded November 23, 1857, at Mendeswor, by a musket-ball, which entered three inches below, and a little internal to the anterior superior spinous process of the ilium, and made exit over the trochanter.

June 28, 1859. Fracture of the left femur at its upper third; bone united; limb $3\frac{1}{4}$ inches shortened; some loose, dead bone can be felt through the unhealed wound of exit; has now a very good, useful limb, and can walk well.

June 29, 1859. Invalided.

This makes 12 undoubted cases of compound comminuted fracture of the femur that have arrived in England during the whole period included in this Report. Of these, 1 died at Gravesend (Walmsley), and 1 (Cunningham) where the cure is complete, but there is considerable deformity of the limb: deducting the death, there remain 11 cases with good, useful limbs out of the total landed, viz., 743, or 1·49 per cent. This is a large proportion compared with the results of the Crimean war, viz., 8 out of 2296, or 0·34 per cent.; and if the case of Moore, which is detailed below, was returned under this head, there would be a total of 13 cases[a].

When the bones of the leg are fractured so as to require

[a] Four cases of gunshot wounds arrived from the war in Persia, all belonging to the 64th Regiment; on the termination of this war the 64th Regiment sailed for Calcutta, and formed part of the force under General Havelock in his advance on Cawnpore and Lucknow. These four cases, although actually wounded in Persia, are included in this return as from the mutiny in India; and one of them, M'Carter, is a case of compound comminuted fracture of the femur.

immediate amputation, this operation will, in all probability, have to be performed in the thigh. If, therefore, a certain number of thigh amputations are admitted, it may be inferred that the greater number had been originally wounds of the leg, and not cases of compound fracture of the femur demanding amputation.

14 amputations of the thigh have arrived from India; of which 13 are returned as in the middle third, and 1 in the upper; or 1·88 per cent. of the total 743 wounded. As stated at page 65, the success of the cases from India with this description of fracture is not to be imputed to the difference of the bullets, but to the better means at hand for treating both compound fractures of the femur and amputations. It also appears to be the better practice not to be over-anxious about the length of the limb, but rather to leave it almost entirely without splints.

In the following case there appears to be some doubt as to whether the femur was actually fractured, or whether it was only a partial fracture; although, from the direction of the ball, and the state of the limb since the injury, there is strong presumptive evidence that there was a complete fracture, either through the neck of the bone or through the trochanter, but without displacement, as now there is almost no shortening, not more, or perhaps so much, as half an inch. This man is, therefore, returned under Class IX., Division 2, but his case is detailed in this place. Of the 12 cases returned there can be no doubt that the femur was fractured.

24th Regt.—Private James Moore, aged 33, thirteen years' service, was wounded by a musket-ball on July 7, 1857, at Jhelum, which entered the left groin, about two inches below Poupart's ligament, and about two and a half inches external to the femoral artery, and passed out an inch and a half behind, and a little below the great trochanter, injuring the bone. Fragments of bone have continued at various times to come away. He has been at Gravesend since August, 1858, since which no dead bone has come away, but "he has had a pretty regular monthly accession of ague," with hepatic complication, lasting for a few days, and followed by formation of matter in the seat of the wound; and sinuses, which have re-opened, discharge for a short time, and then quite heal up, to break out again on the next disturbance of the general health. There is now considerable phlegmonous inflammation around the wound and whole of upper part of thigh, and necrosed bone exists in considerable quantity. General health good.

Class XI.—Gunshot Wounds, with direct Penetration or Perforation of the larger Joints.

Two cases were admitted, viz., one of the elbow-joint, which is now anchylosed; but the patient has a very useful hand: the other was in the knee. The following is the history of the case:—

14th Light Dragoons.—Private James Ball, aged 30, was wounded at Muddenpore Pass on 3rd March, 1858, by a musket-ball, which entered the outer side of left knee, and was cut out about two inches posteriorly. Joint primarily injured? The surgeon says, No; but the contrary seems probable. Free incisions around the joint were subsequently required. The limb can now only be flexed to a slight extent, but the joint has lateral motion in a direction inwards to middle line.

Invalided June 29, 1859.

Class XII.—Gunshot Wounds with direct Injury of the larger Nerves, not being at the same time cases of Compound Fracture.

2 were admitted, and 1 sent to duty.

42nd Regt.—Sergeant Joseph Mumford, aged 28, on March 11, 1858, received a wound from a musket-bullet (round), which entered about an inch and a half from the sternal articulation of the clavicle of right side, and was extracted from the left side of the neck behind, about the centre of the clavicle. The trachea was injured, and he spat blood for seven or eight days, and the air came out through the hole of entrance. The cervical plexus has been injured; the trachea, in the course of the wound, is tender, the opening of exit very much so, and all the fingers appear quite useless: they are fixed, apparently anchylosed in a straight position, but any attempt at bending them causes intense pain in the course of the median nerve. The hand is cold, and affected with nervous tremor; all the fingers are numb, but the motions and sensation of the thumb are good.

May, 1859. Duty. Results of wound probably not to a disqualifying extent.

Pl. XI.

G. H. Ford. W. West imp.

APPENDIX.

PLATE XI. represents the description of dooley which is used for the conveyance of the sick and wounded in India. The dooley forms in the field the patient's bed, as well as means of conveyance from the time of his being wounded until he is either cured or the case terminates fatally. There are two dooley-bearers in front, and two behind, with the reliefs; they generally carry the dooley from ten to fourteen miles' march a day. When they arrive at the encampment, they run the dooley into the hospital tent, take out the pole with the tarpaulin covering and curtains, and then leave the patients comfortably in their beds; the following morning, at a certain hour, the bearers return with their bamboo pole and the top of the dooley, put them on in a minute, and start for the next halting-place. The roofs of two dooleys placed together form a shade for the bearers at night, and during the heat of the day. During the Crimean war Deputy-Inspector J. R. Taylor, C. B., who has had great experience in India, and also in Europe, recommended a dooley corps. Sir George Ballingall, in his "Military Surgery," Fourth Edition, page 106, says: "Nothing can well be conceived more perfectly adapted to the conveyance of sick than the dooley;" and I shall only further quote the words of an Indian medical officer, Superintending-Surgeon Charles Renny, in his "Report on the Medical Arrangements of the Army of the Punjaub during the campaign of 1848–9:" "The dooley is the most comfortable conveyance for a wounded or sick person; it cannot be replaced by anything better." And this seems to be the opinion both of medical officers and also of military officers who have served in India, and are, therefore, qualified to judge.

It would be too expensive, and perhaps an unnecessary measure to have, as in India, one dooley and dooley-bearers for each regiment, or even for battalions at home in time of peace; still, a suitable supply of dooleys might be procured from India, and placed in store until required in the event of war, when bearers could be immediately called for from India for this duty.

The best dooley-bearers generally come from the country round Cawnpore and the lower provinces, and, though natives of such a hot country, are surely as able to serve in the capacity of bearer in a European climate as the British soldier is able to serve as such in the Bengal climate. There should be eight bearers to each dooley, with the usual number of sirdars, mate-bearers, and mussalchees; they should be enlisted, have extra pay for foreign service, and be entitled to a pension on beingsent back to India, disable d by disease or injury.

THE END.